The Management of Luck

An Original Guide to Business Success

The Management of Luck

An Original Guide to Business Success

JOHN BURKE

In association with
Graham Jones
of Writers in Business

Macdonald

A Macdonald Book

Copyright © John Burke 1989
Illustrations copyright © Bud Handelsman 1989

First published in Great Britain in 1989 by
Macdonald & Co (Publishers) Ltd
London & Sydney

British Library Cataloguing in Publication Data

Burke, John
The management of luck
1.Management
I.Title
658
ISBN 0-356-15544-7

Photoset in North Wales by
Derek Doyle & Associates, Mold, Clwyd.
Printed in Great Britain by
Redwood Burn Limited, Trowbridge, Wiltshire
Bound at the Dorstel Press

Macdonald & Co (Publishers) Ltd
66-73 Shoe Lane
London EC4P 4AB
A member of Maxwell Pergamon Publishing Corporation plc

For Alex and John,
two pieces of real luck.

'Chance favours the mind that is prepared.'
Louis Pasteur

PREFACE

IN 1986, while I was at Glaxo, we produced a drug for the treatment of cardiovascular disease. A few days before the launch in Rome, two things happened. Edwina Currie, the British Junior Health Minister, created a splash in the papers by speaking out on the dangers of the disease and the fact that more should be done to tackle it. (What most drew the attention of journalists was her criticism of eating habits in the North of England, but we happily forgave her that.) The second event was Bill Asher, Chairman of the Committee for the Safety of Medicines, going on national radio and ramming home the same message.

When we got to Rome, we found high admiration for the way we had engineered events. All that media attention, perfectly timed for the launch – how had we done it?

In fact we had done nothing. We'd been lucky. That said, our good fortune was not entirely due to luck. Long beforehand, Glaxo had identified cardiovascular disease as one of the most seriously undertreated ailments in the western world. It was not surprising, therefore, that politicians and others should come to the same conclusion at about that time. But for both events to have happened just days before the launch – that was lucky. Our task, then, was to make the most of the luck that had befallen us.

After twenty years in management, I am convinced that there is no such thing as undiluted luck: management nearly always creeps into it somewhere. Nor is there such a thing as pure management, for there is always an element of chance. That being so, it can only make better managers of us to examine the relationship between management and luck. After all, management is most interesting when it is dealing with the unexpected, with chance, with change – and never has change been more rapid or unpredictable than in the industrialised world of the late twentieth century.

This book attempts to put luck and management together and to see how they fit. I think it is timely to do so, for most management books have nothing whatever to say on luck. You read them and think, 'That's all very interesting, but unless that particular bit of luck comes *my* way, I can't begin to engage. What I need is a way of manufacturing some luck.'

That's not as bizarre a notion as it may sound. I believe it can be done, and this book explains how. There's no magic here. Reading this book will not make you rich, slim, happy, beautiful, famous or successful. However, it will demonstrate how casting a different light on your business will put you in greater command of events taking place around you.

What I have to say is culled from twenty years in the pharmaceutical industry in Europe and the United States. Born and brought up in a Lancashire mill town, I have worked for the British companies, ICI and Beecham, and for two American giants, G.D. Searle and Merck Sharp and Dohme. This book was conceived and most of it written while I was Chairman of Glaxo Pharmaceuticals.

I've had some lucky breaks, of course, but no more than average. All I'd say is, I've tried to make the most of the luck that has come my way. In the course of so doing I've learned what I think are some important lessons on luck and management. This book spells them out.

John V. Burke
100, Piccadilly,
June 1988

CHAPTER ONE

A Funny Little Thing Called Luck

THE PHONE rang one Monday morning in 1981. At the time I was General Manager of G.D. Searle in High Wycombe, and as usual on a Monday morning I was sorting out the job list for the week. It looked like being a busy few days. The caller was the Secretary of the Chemical Society.

'I'd like to know if you could give a talk to the Society,' he began, giving me a date a few weeks further on.

I glanced at the in-tray. It contained the tangle of challenges and problems I thought I'd be addressing that week. Now, cutting across my bows, came this new request.

Now I'm not one who can lecture off the cuff. However well I know the subject, an hour on the platform takes at least five hours' preparation. Quite apart from working out what to say, I can't rest easy unless I go in ahead of time and research the battlefield. I like to know where the switch is on the overhead projector, to test the blackout, and generally cover myself against every contingency. This invitation would gobble up swathes of time that I knew I couldn't spare. My first thought was to say no, get the Secretary of the Chemical Society off the phone, and get on with the week. Instead, without really meaning to, I asked him what the subject was.

'We've got three topics,' he continued. 'Preparing for the Worst, Riding the Storm and Good Luck and Good Management.'

'I pity the poor devil who gets the third,' I replied. The title was a contradiction – too much like squaring the circle for my liking. You'd need a PhD in metaphysics to get a grip on that one, I thought.

There was a pause from the other end. 'I'm sorry to say, that's the only topic left.'

Five hours when I know the subject … How many hours to wrestle a cock-eyed topic such as this into some presentable form? My mind tracked ahead trying to find the time in a crowded diary. It looked impossible. I knew I couldn't do it.

'I'll do it,' I said.

That lecture was the hardest I've ever prepared. Good luck and good management? Like oil and water, they seemed impossible to mix. Luck is what cannot be managed; management, by definition, stops short of luck. I realized I had committed myself to talking intelligently on how to control the uncontrollable.

Resorting to my dictionary and thesaurus took me no further forward. I fell into the pages carrying 'luck' hoping I would be lucky/fortunate/fortuitously helped to find an angle with which I could comfortably deal. I was unlucky. Among alien words like 'voodoo', 'rabbit's foot', 'amulet' and 'talisman', the definition lurked uncompromisingly: 'Luck – the fancied tendency of chance.' Flicking to the other word in the title gave no comfort: 'Manage – have effective control of.'

How does a working manager take effective control of the fancied tendency of chance? No management book I knew had even addressed the problem, let alone solved it.

When stuck, it never hurts to examine the problem from the other end. Instead of worrying about how we manage luck, let us suppose ourselves in a world in which luck manages us. The computer operator in the next room ceases to work methodically and instead plunges across the keys at random, hoping his cashflow projection will materialize like the works of Shakespeare from one of those mythical monkeys. Think further. The computer at which he sits will have been assembled by nimble-footed operatives kicking pieces across the factory floor until a working machine appears. Or perhaps not. In a world truly controlled by luck, the owner of the computer factory will send his workers home, shut down the business and retire to the nearest field in the expectation that food, clothing and the rest of life's necessities will fall from the sky or be blown across the terrain from passing lorries. If there are lorries in such a world.

Perhaps there's a chink in the logic that luck and management do not mix. Instead of defining luck as that which cannot be controlled, let us view it as that to which we *give* control. By expedients such as building a factory, designing a computer or following the instructions in a manual, we shrink the territory governed by luck and increase the probability that what we want to happen will happen.

The same might be said of every human action, from putting on a shirt to preparing a five-year plan. Push the argument a little further, and life itself is about converting chance into order.

By implication, therefore, good management is about increasing your powers of control and reducing the element of luck as much as you can. This in turn implies that some things are brought under control that were previously thought to be uncontrollable – fortuitous, random, without pattern. To have given in and labelled them 'luck' would have been a mistake. Luck has a movable borderline. The good manager keeps his eye on it and tries to move it back.

However, however...we cannot eradicate luck. Every manager knows he is never in total control; that somewhere there exists the probability co-efficient (the smart way of saying 'the unpredictable'). Nor, I trust, would we want to be rid of luck. There are those who try their hardest – the logicians who grind luck away and nibble at what remains. But they grind away the fun as well. Life stripped of chance would be unbearably dull. On the other hand, a breezy acceptance of chance is no way to run a business. I've known managers who frighten you to death by selling out to luck and saying it's all right as long as it works 51 per cent of the time.

There has to be a balance. Push back the boundary, but recognize you won't push it all the way. Don't deny the label 'luck', but refuse to attach it until you have thrown the net of management as wide as you can. But once we've done that, what do we do with the luck that remains? I make two suggestions. First of all, avoid calling it good or bad. Secondly, turn it to your advantage.

It's worth a few lines to scotch the epithets 'good' and 'bad' in relation to luck.

To begin with, quick labelling is the refuge of the lazy. To call something luck when it isn't saves the trouble both of thinking and of taking control where control is possible. As soon as mankind coined the word 'luck' he was able to abandon himself to almost anything. And it's the same with the epithets. 'It's my bad luck I'm only a platelayer on British Rail when I could have been running ICI' sounds like surrender: at least, it puts the blame elsewhere. And to toss off success as 'good luck' does you no service either. Success has ingredients: much of it – maybe all of it – is a consequence of people, yourself and others, either doing things or not doing things. The label is an excuse. It saves analysis. It denies you the possibility of marshalling the same circumstances again and carrying your success further.

Secondly, the epithets 'good' and 'bad' are shot through with subjectivity. Marshal Ney, so the story goes, survived Waterloo but had four horses killed under him during the battle. 'How lucky,' we might say. I demur. You could just as well call it bad luck. How many months' wages does a horse cost? Or what about Roy Sullivan, the human lightning conductor of Virginia? According to the Guinness Book of Records, he was struck by lightning seven times between 1942 and 1977 and lived to tell the tale. What amazing luck! Or was it? I don't think I would swap with Mr Sullivan, even for a place in the famous book.

Thirdly, it's everybody's experience that so-called 'good

luck' frequently turns into 'bad luck' and vice versa. 'It was bad luck I missed the train … but five minutes later I met my old friend Jim on the platform.' 'It was good luck I got to be a director … what a pity I never have time for my children.' It's impossible to apply either epithet with confidence until the whole picture is known – and when is that? This year? Next year? The day you die?

Fourthly, every use of the terms 'good luck' and 'bad luck' implies a criterion – something desired that good luck helps us towards and bad luck denies us. And what is that criterion to be? Career success? Physical comfort? Home and family? Self-integration? The climber, Norman Croucher, fell under a train at the age of nineteen and lost both his legs below the knee. Bad luck? You would hardly call it good. Now, instead of being one of a million climbers with real legs, he's one of a tiny elite with artificial legs. He has written a book, been voted Man of the Year, become a member of the Sports Council and generally achieved in areas he never thought were open to him. Now whether he would trade all that for his legs back, I cannot say: it would be impertinent to presume. But again and again, a new angle on so-called bad luck transmutes it into something different.

Alexander Solzhenitsyn, who spent years in Stalin's labour camps, wrote this: 'I turn back to the years of my imprisonment and say, sometimes to the astonishment of those about me, "Bless you, prison." '

In short, good luck and bad luck have a way of turning inside out.

But I'm straying into metaphysics…issues of why we're here and what is ultimately good for us. I step sharply back, leaving the field to priests, philosophers and psychologists. This is a practical book for managers. The 'good' in our context is your career and how to make the most of it: nothing more. Nevertheless, a glimpse over the rim confirms that 'good luck' and 'bad luck' are inherently wobbly concepts, quite apart from distracting managers from the task of managing.

Life deals out circumstance – and circumstance becomes good luck or bad depending on how it is handled.

I make one proviso. There exists a kind of bad luck (a better word is tragedy) before which one can only sit in silence and hope that the victim has something to cling to. Just as we cannot squeeze chance entirely out of the picture, so we must allow room for plain rotten circumstance. And this book, I have to say it, is not for people whom life has disabled. It's for those who have the ability to move further and do better if they view their circumstances from a new position. And a large part of that is to jettison the 'good-luck bad-luck' mentality.

Management and luck do not mix: the title remains a contradiction in terms. But the way through the conundrum is to alter the ratio – to recognize the million ways we abandon ourselves to fate, and to realize that life is often more manageable than we think. Having minimized chance as best we can, the key is to switch, chameleon-like, and become an opportunist – in other words, to maximize the chance that remains.

How to do that was the theme of my lecture.

CHAPTER TWO

Four Essential Qualities

THE GOOD manager minimizes chance and makes the most of the chance remaining. The question is how.

The answer – as in most things – lies in people. It is people, after all, who make things happen. No scientific discovery was ever made, no widget ever produced, no book ever printed unless people did something. With the exception of acts of God, luck can be no more than a function of homo sapiens.

So let us 'people-orientate'. Let us cast the question differently and ask, 'What would be the characteristics of a manager who could minimize chance and maximize the chance remaining?'

This was the question I set myself as I began preparing my Chemical Society lecture. In no time at all the list of likely characteristics had stretched beyond thirty – too many to be helpful. I had to cut back, and began to realize that all were aspects of four central qualities. The good manager of luck is the one who will exercise:

awareness,
judgement,
courage and
flexibility.

Since 1981 I have lectured on the management of luck several times a year, and people are constantly saying, 'You've missed one out ... what about this one?' Opportunism, for example, is often singled out as missing from the list. But if you think about it, the opportunist combines all four of those qualities. He's *aware* of something happening and *judges* how to respond: he often exercises *courage*, and he's nothing if not *flexible*. Seven years on I'm convinced that these four qualities are elemental. I have not been able to make do with less, nor have I found another quality that is not based on one or more of them.

This book, therefore, is about awareness, judgement, courage and flexibility, and how they help you to manage luck. Before we look at them in detail, let me offer the brief account of each as it appeared in my lecture all those years ago.

AWARENESS

We have to be aware that events have happened, are happening, are about to happen, if we are to turn as much luck as we can into planning.

If you did not make yourself aware of the dermatological effects of the chemicals your staff handled, and this caused injuries that in turn damaged your labour relations, you could hardly put it down to bad luck. The fault would lie in your awareness – or lack of it.

You must also ascertain whether what you have discovered is good news or bad news – or whether it will have no effect on the business at all. It's my contention that almost nothing in life comes pre-tagged as good or bad luck. So don't just gather information; turn it round, examine it from every angle and work out the full implications. Only by so doing can you fully exploit what luck happens to bring you.

So how do we build up good awareness?

One: by recruiting people of dedication, diligence and resourcefulness – people, in other words, who will raise the level of corporate awareness.

Two: make ample use of market and marketing research. I distinguish between the two: one is strategy, the other tactics. Market research studies the size, shape, dynamics and trends of the market in question. Marketing research deals with the tactical deployment of resources in those markets.

Three: maintain a good library and an efficient press service. Make sure you have all the relevant facts about your industry, your company, your competitors …

In every company, employee A will have in his head information which, if known to employee B, would benefit the business. So a fourth prerequisite for good awareness is an environment that encourages freedom of speech, openness and the exchange of data and ideas.

JUDGEMENT

Having made yourself aware, analyze what your awareness tells you and plan accordingly. Naturally, good corporate judgement requires good people. It needs the right combination of linear thinkers (those who contribute rigid logic and scrupulous protocols to the problem) and lateral minds that can view from many angles. It also, of course, needs people with experience.

Experience is an interesting case. It's not an extra quality to the four I've postulated, but a fusion of them all. If, over time, your awareness has broadened and your judgement become sharper, you'll probably exercise courage and flexibility with greater ease. But experience should not be confused with time-serving. It's a function of two things – your exposure to people and events, and your willingness to benefit from that exposure. I've come across people who are more 'experienced' after six months in a job than colleagues who have been there twenty years.

Inevitably, awareness and judgement overlap with courage and flexibility, our two remaining headings. Faintheartedness can definitely impair judgement. So can a situation where sheer bravery overwhelms the individual's analytical prowess.

The best *living* motor racers have judgement and bravery well balanced. A gap between the two means either you keep losing races or you go to an early grave. But now we're moving from the minimization of chance to the point where we have done all we can and must make the most of what fate gives us. This is where courage and flexibility become relevant.

COURAGE

In my experience, bad luck often forces people into action. Something adverse has happened; you could not have foreseen it; you are pressed into a response. The courage element is nil, for you have done what you had to do, not what you chose to do. On the other hand, the brave response – founded on awareness and judgement – might well be to do nothing.

It is the reverse with good luck. To enlarge it into more good luck, rather than letting it wash over you in the finite volume in which it was delivered, usually requires action. In this case action is not imposed on you. You volunteer it at your peril, and the only saving grace is getting it right.

Imagine you are MD of Babybounce, a retail chain catering for the needs of infants and young children. After years of static population, a stroke of luck (from your point of view if nobody else's) comes your way. A solar wind bathes the earth and fertility increases a thousandfold. The effect is not instantly apparent, for population statistics are based on births, not pregnancies. Nevertheless, your corporate awareness machine picks up the fact that pregnancies are running at a far higher rate than normal. You judge, correctly, that demand for nappies will rise by a thousandfold in six months' time.

Are you then brave enough to go before the board and say you want to increase capacity in the nappy factory 1000 times at a time when the figures are still incredible? Can you go against the prejudices and doubts of your colleagues and get

them to be brave as well?

We cannot, I think, alter the basic level of courage with which we are born or which we have acquired by the time we reach employment. But we can, as managers, draw out the courage in others – by dealing fairly; by balancing praise and criticism; by encouraging people at least to try; and by offering proper reward.

FLEXIBILITY

The key now is to maximize what luck has brought you, and this means flexibility. Is your organization capable of overhauling its plans overnight? If it comes to it, is your production unit able to produce millions more nappies each week?

As chance overtakes our precautions to minimize its effects, we may have to turn ourselves upside down. Flexibility can mean working on Sunday or not working on Wednesday; it can mean working non-stop for six months, or learning a language, or getting a pilot's licence.... In any event, it is a change of course, with all the anxiety, discomfort and excitement that change so often entails.

So to summarize, you manage your luck by pushing back the boundary between that which you control and that which you don't, and you do so by exercising *awareness* and *judgement*. But of course you can never fully control your luck. Acknowledging that the unexpected will always creep in somewhere, you need *courage* and *flexibility* to reduce the effect of bad luck and make the most of the good.

In a sentence, you minimise chance, then maximise the chance that remains.

If

by Rudyard Kipling

If you can keep your head when all about you
Are losing theirs and blaming it on you,
If you can trust yourself when all men doubt you,
But make allowance for their doubting too;
If you can wait and not be tired of waiting,
Or being lied about, don't deal in lies,
Or being hated, don't give way to hating,
And yet don't look too good, nor talk too wise:

If you can dream – and not make dreams your master;
If you can think – and not make thoughts your aim;
If you can meet with Triumph and Disaster
And treat those two imposters just the same;
If you can bear to hear the truth you've spoken
Twisted by knaves to make a trap for fools,
Or watch the things you gave your life to, broken,
And stoop and build 'em up with worn-out tools:

If you can make one heap of all your winnings
And risk it on one turn of pitch-and-toss,
And lose, and start again at your beginnings
And never breathe a word about your loss;
If you can force your heart and nerve and sinew
To serve your turn long after they are gone,
And so hold on when there is nothing in you
Except the Will which says to them: 'Hold on!'

If you can talk with crowds and keep your virtue,
Or walk with Kings – nor lose the common touch,
If neither foes nor loving friends can hurt you,
If all men count with you, but none too much;
If you can fill the unforgiving minute
With sixty seconds' worth of distance run,
Yours is the Earth and everything that's in it,
And – which is more – you'll be a Man, my son.

CHAPTER THREE

When Grandad Fell Down A Hole

THE GOOD manager of luck is the one who exhibits awareness, judgement, courage and flexibility. But let us ask the question, 'What kind of person is it who can exercise those qualities?'

The face that comes to my mind, surprisingly, is not that of a manager at all. It's the shrewd, obstinate face of an Irishman in his late sixties. It is in fact my grandfather as I remember him in the mid-1950s – I being little more than ten at the time.

Grandfather was his own man, and that made all the difference when he fell down a hole that someone had left uncovered in the pavement. Now there is nothing more purely unlucky than falling down a hole, though I concede that a little more awareness on his part might have prevented it happening in the first place. From the moment he climbed out of the hole with a painfully broken shoulder, Grandad was determined to turn circumstance to his favour.

His own father had been born in Ireland and had come to Manchester during The Troubles. He set up the city's very first motor-coach company and made a great deal of money taking early trippers to Blackpool by road. I still have a picture of the old man with his three-piece suit, big red nose and magnificent Edwardian moustache, standing proudly by one of his vehicles. The family never saw the money he made because he drank it almost as quickly as he made it. Night after night they'd bring him home in a handcart, and a sovereign to the local bobby would usually be enough to keep him out of the police cells. His wife, my great-grandmother, kept a jar with corks in the kitchen cupboard in case his Irish temper got the better of him. When that happened, he'd rip the gas fittings out of the ceiling, and the corks were to prevent the family from being gassed until the plumber arrived.

Great-grandad was not educated; I'm not even sure he was literate; but he was an extremely shrewd judge of people and events. If nothing else, he knew the value of a sovereign to a poorly paid policeman. And Grandad, with little education himself, inherited that shrewdness. When the coach business collapsed, he went off into the next best thing which was haulage, and for the rest of his working life pottered from one job to another. At the time he fell down the hole he was semi-retired and working for *The Daily Express* as a nightwatchman. It was in the course of his rounds one night that the accident happened.

Shrewd man that he was, he knew from reading the newspapers and the chat that he picked up in the pub that leaving holes in pavements was not on. He judged that somebody was responsible and could therefore be made to pay. My father and uncle told him not to be a damned old fool, to get better and forget about it. But Grandad was determined – courageous, indeed, in the face of the family's opposition. He werrited, as they'd say in Lancashire. He worried and nattered and nagged and probed, talking to this person and that person and picking up all the advice he could over pints of Boddingtons at the Queen's Hotel (or it might have been The Junction – he frequented both). Eventually he acquired enough confidence in his case to take it to a solicitor. For a man of his background, that was a formidable undertaking. It needed extraordinary flexibility as it meant moving into circles he'd never previously entered.

With no help, and vigorously resisted by the rest of the

You definitely have a case, Mr. Burke.
I'm cold sober, and what's more I don't buy it by the case.

family, he won his case and was awarded £635 against *The Daily Express*. That was about a year's pay for my father and several years' pay for Grandad. He generously gave his two sons £100 each, and that money was the deposit on the first home my father ever bought.

I think it ran in the family. Grandad won his case because he knew he had a point and would not be deflected. My father, too, was his own man, but his creed was more conscious and formalized than Grandad's. The poem of my youth was Rudyard Kipling's 'If'. My father knew it by heart and would quote it at salient points in my upbringing. I grew up learning to recite it and imbued with its stern criteria for manhood.

The message of the poem, it seems to me, is self-sufficiency and balance – being your own man and steering your own course between extremes. My father's philosophy was much influenced by its thirty-two lines. You are no better or worse, my son, than the next man. Regardless of your background, your accent or whether or not your house has electricity, you are that man's equal. Respect him, but also know that you deserve his respect.

As a child, of course, one is never fully conscious of parental influence at work. But I do remember the discovery that my father's philosophy had taken root. It was the day I met the ICI Research Director.

I was eighteen at the time and in my first job at the ICI laboratory in Manchester. I worked at a bench in a laboratory, and down the middle of the bench was a shaft with pulley wheels, kept in constant rotation by an electric motor under the sink. If you had an experiment that needed stirring, you simply hooked a band round one of these pulley wheels and there you had a full-time stirring mechanism.

One day the motor failed and my boss was nowhere to be seen. So at lunchtime, when I'd had my sandwiches, I took the end off the sink unit, went down to my motorbike, brought my toolkit up and fixed it. Later in the afternoon a man rolled up demanding to know where the fault was.

'It's all right,' I said, 'I've mended it.'

At this, all hell was let loose because I'd contravened the standard procedure. My boss, I now know, had gone off at lunchtime to set the procedure in motion. When properly observed, it used to work like this. Once a fault was reported, a man in a suit would arrive – as he duly had done – and ask, 'Where is the fault?' You'd show him and he'd go away. Two days later, a man in a boiler suit but with no tools would arrive and say, 'Where is the fault?' You'd show him and he, too, would go away. The next day a younger man in a boiler suit, this time with a tool bag, would arrive, leave his tools and disappear. A day later the two men in boiler suits would arrive and repair the fault. The day after that the man in the suit and the original chap in the boiler suit would come along and make sure the job had been done. The following day, at least a week after the breakdown allowing for weekends, the young man in the boiler suit would come and take the tools away.

In repairing the motor in twenty minutes over lunch, I had contravened every demarcation rule in the union book. Such was the storm that arose, that when the sink became blocked a couple of weeks later, I wouldn't have unblocked it myself for a gold clock. Indeed, if it had become unblocked, I would probably have bunged it up again before anyone arrived.

It was on the day of this second mishap, the blocked sink, that my father's philosophy proved its worth. I was busying myself with my experiments when a gentleman I'd never seen before turned up and started pottering around the desk. Noting that he wore a suit, I stood by for the expected question: 'Where is the fault?' The man didn't speak. It was getting towards the end of the day, so I toured the desk checking my experiments and stabilizing everything for the night.

Eventually it was time to go, so I interrupted his potterings. 'Have you come to unblock the sink?' I asked.

He turned out to be the ICI Research Director, as lofty a figure as anyone in my position could imagine. My mother's attitude in those circumstances would have been one of great discomfort and reverence. The opposite reaction – the one you'd expect, perhaps, from a boy of eighteen – would have been to overcompensate for my nervousness by being truculent. But my father's influence took me right down the middle. Faced with this great man and my own *faux pas*, I found to my surprise that I wasn't at all nervous. I didn't feel inferior; nor did I feel the need to be belligerent. The man was a fine chemist: I'm sure he had forgotten more chemistry than I will ever know. But that didn't make the person any better or worse. With the gift of detachment my father had bequeathed, I found I could look at him with completely objective respect.

This unbiased regard for the individual has stood me in good stead ever since. Ironically, my father found it more difficult to practise than I have done, for it never sat comfortably with his strong sympathy for trade unions.

Ours was very much a union household. The big event of the month was the arrival of a large brown package containing copies of *The Draughtsman* and *The Vacancy List*. It came from my father's union, and one of his duties as local branch secretary was to roll up the magazines, push them into little tubes, stick on hundreds of address labels and post them. As a small boy I had no idea what was going on, but they made an impressive sight, and a highlight in my life was taking them across the road in carrier bags to post them.

Father was a socialist, a reader of *The Daily Herald*. In that mould, he could never come to terms with people like Tommy Arnold. Tommy was seen to be 'in management'. He lived in a larger, newer terraced house four hundred yards away. At best he was a senior clerk, but he was white-collar. With no children, Tommy and his wife were comfortable. The differences were tiny but palpable. Tommy was the other side of the tracks and that was that.

Given the family background, I was quite prepared to be a union man when I joined ICI. However, doubts set in the first week I was there when the union representative came round with the papers. He was an unkempt, spindly young man with dry hair and buck teeth. I can see him now – very weak, very wet, bleary-faced with smears of sleep in the corners of his eyes. I began to wonder why a man like this should be seeking a common cause with me. 'Who would be supporting whom?' I asked myself. I then found as I started asking questions that his argument didn't stack up. Trying to discover what the union's policies were, I got cant. Even when my questions became more altruistic – 'What can I do for the union?' – the answer was to pay my dues. So somebody else had worked it out. All that was wanted was my money and my membership as a head. The union could then vote using J. Burke as number 308 and J. Burke would have no power to change the vote even if he disagreed.

Union membership, I decided then, was a kind of emasculation. It would take away my identity, my freedom of action. I could not do it, and have never been a union member to this day. Don't get me wrong: I'm not personally anti-union. It's simply that the unions I encountered in the early '60s were decades out of date, their attitudes and practices more suited to a labour-intensive, smoke-stack era than to a modern industry such as pharmaceuticals. In the intervening years the pendulum has corrected itself, I believe, and today's unions are more responsive to the real needs of their members.

At the time I was starting my career my father was also having doubts about union membership. It became clear to him over time that Kipling's 'If' philosophy was incompatible with mass solidarity. On the one hand, 'Be your own man; nobody does anything for you; if you don't put effort in you'll get nothing out.' On the other hand, 'Throw in your lot with the union; let the union use its leverage to get you what you want … but remember that the payrise will also be applied to a million other people – the skivers as well as those who deserve it.'

My father came from Cheetham Hill, the Jewish-Catholic quarter of Manchester, and made his way through life with no formal qualifications. My childhood memories are of a stern, humourless man, though I realize now that his humour was of the dry, deadpan variety that is lost on children. The Edwardian, Catholic stamp was firmly on him: I don't think he learned to laugh until he was middle-aged. His mother put him out originally as a tailor's apprentice. Then the chance came – and he seized it – to join the engineering firm, A.V. Roe, known as AVRO. Somebody took him under his wing and taught him to be a design draughtsman. He was a very good one, designing, among other things, some of the machine tools that made components for the Lancaster bomber. His progress was steady, if undramatic, and he eventually became Chief Engineer and Factory Manager at Ferranti.

As he climbed the management scale, he began to see the other side of the industrial equation. The company had to survive. The holding down of salaries was not management parsimony but a function of the need to be competitive. In any case,

> 'If you can force your heart and nerve and sinew
> > To serve your turn ...'

who needs the union? In the end, Kipling won and my father gave up his union membership.

Two further events in my early career confirmed for me that trusting yourself is generally a better policy than throwing in your lot with a union. Both occurred after I had left ICI and was working as a technical representative for a firm that manufactured printing inks.

Mars, the makers of the well known chocolate bar, had invented Opal Fruits, and a printing firm in Liverpool was bidding for the contract to supply the packaging. Then, as now, the tube was illustrated with varieties of fruit in full colour – a virtuoso piece of print involving five-colour, photo-gravure offset on foil. A man called Batchelor ran the printing firm. It was his own company and he'd put in a lot of hard work to win the chance to tender.

The day came when the senior managers of Mars arrived on site to see what he could do for them. I was one of the three technicians waiting in the wings in case anything went wrong. The workers loaded the ink into the presses, the rollers were put in, the paper was run up to tension and the first proofs were taken. Everything looked good. We were ready to demonstrate. Batchelor, dressed in his best suit, emerged from the boardroom with his visitors and led them to the gantry above the press. The plan was that the presses would run and Batchelor would tear off a sample to present to the gentlemen from Mars. He pressed the button. But instead of the presses rolling, the union representative blew a whistle and the entire workforce walked out on strike.

I thought, 'They're crazy! Surely they're damaging themselves!' Looking back on the incident now, I still feel the same. These were not people minimizing luck and maximizing opportunity: they were distorting the normal dynamics of industry and economics to give themselves an artificial slice of life's desirables. 'If I can't have my Ford Cortina, my TV and my Spanish holiday, I'll take it out on somebody and it might as well be management because they've got clean hands, clean suits, better cars and bigger mortgages.'

The second episode happened at about the same time.

My job as a technical rep meant spending time in the laboratory formulating inks, doing tests and solving problems thrown up in the marketplace. One such problem was the fact that Beecham's powder contains cinnamon oil, and cinnamon oil lifts the ink off almost anything. To get the Beecham account, we had to produce an ink that would resist this effect. And it wasn't enough to solve the problem in a test tube: the solution had to work day in, day out on printing presses up and down the land. That meant travelling out to printing firms to see how the ink performed.

I forget why, but the unions in the company fell out with the management and went on strike. On the first day of the strike, I turned up to collect my samples, intending to take them off and test them to see if we'd cracked Beecham's problem.

Billy the Picket was keeping guard at the warehouse door. 'Keeping guard' is perhaps the wrong term. He and a couple of others were playing poker on an upturned, 40-gallon solvents drum. Billy – despite the hazard from the solvents – was rolling his own and smoking as he played. I asked respectfully if they would let me past to collect my samples.

'You can't have them,' said Billy, barely shifting his eyes from the game.

'Why not?'

'We're on strike.'

'Well, that's all right, Bill,' I said. 'I'm not on strike.'

'Yes, but you're undermining the strike.'

'No, I'm not,' I persisted. 'I'm not manufacturing any ink. I'm taking some samples to go sixty miles to Blackburn to do some trials. You won't see me for a week. When you and management have sorted out your differences, I'll be back with some orders and we'll all be happy.'

No go. They wouldn't let me in. So I waited until they were otherwise occupied at lunchtime and went and got what I needed. Back from Blackburn at the end of the week, I was taken round the back of the bikesheds, lectured, threatened, and lightly roughed up. The physical damage was nil, but the offence was total.

I applaud the unionism that protects the poor and exploited. What I deplore is unionism that distorts the laws of economics through sheer weight of numbers. My quarrel, I think, is not even with unionism but with any kind of collectivism. Collective man – be he out on strike, pouring into a football ground or even sitting at a desk preserving his position through mutual solidarity with his colleagues – is not a pretty sight. What is more, bolstered by numbers, he tends to get away with more than his due. So what I say of unionism (and I mean the outdated unionism that I encountered twenty years ago) goes for other forms of collectivism too.

My main objection is that joining a union makes it more difficult to manage your own luck.

In the extreme case, it means abandoning awareness: from now on the union bosses will tell you what you need to know. It means letting go of judgement. Making up your own mind is inappropriate, as I discovered behind the bikesheds.

In any case, you cannot make judgements on a faulty database: no awareness, no judgement. You've also sold your courage into a corporate pool and you're relying now on someone else's bravery to secure your ends. And not least, you lose your flexibility.

'Go and stand in the car park,' says Billy the Picket or one of his ilk.

'Why?'

'Never you mind.'

I come back to my grandfather's example. To be your own man, you must be responsible for your own awareness and the judgements you make on the basis of that awareness. You cannot abandon your flexibility and you cannot sell your courage to someone else.

In short, you cannot take charge of luck if you're not in charge of yourself.

CHAPTER FOUR

I Found I'd Been Doing It All My Life

'GOOD MORNING sir, I wonder if I could interest you in purchasing a vacuum cleaner.' It was an August day in 1954. The salesman stood at the door of my parents' terraced house in Oldham, his bakelite machine in a large hold-all under his arm.

My father was a terror to doorstep callers. If they were Jehovah's Witnesses, he said he was a Catholic. If the parish priest came round, he claimed to be a Jehovah's Witness. Anyone resembling a sleeked-down, brush-cum-encyclopaedia salesman – as this man certainly did – got very short shrift from my father. 'Not interested,' he said, and started to close the door.

'Half a mo',' protested the man. 'At least let me show you. It's a lovely machine.'

'I guarantee,' said my father gravely, 'you'll never sell me a vacuum cleaner.'

'I guarantee I can if you let me in.'

My father thought for a moment, then swung open the door and showed him into the little front room. The first thing the salesman did was to take a square of carpet from his bag and lay it on the floor. He then produced a little bag of dust and rubbish and scattered the contents carefully over the square. All the while he was chattering to my father who watched him in silence.

'I'm taking the precaution of using my sample of carpet, sir, though I assure you that when you see the results you wouldn't bat an eyelid, even were I to use your own carpet.' He rubbed his hands in anticipation. 'Righto, I think we're ready. Where's yer power point.'

'We haven't got one,' said my father.

' 'Aven't...? Yer mean...?'

My father nodded. 'No electricity. I said you'd never sell me a vacuum cleaner.'

He was decent enough after that to lend the salesman a dustpan and brush to sweep up the muck. (If ever there was a case of courage overwhelming awareness, this salesman exemplified it.) My father enjoyed the episode enormously and told the story often. And it was true, we had no electricity, no hot water system and no bathroom until I was twelve.

For the first four years of my life we lived, the three of us, in the back bedroom of my maternal grandmother's house next door to Tommy Arnold. From there we moved to a tiny, end-of-terrace house on the main A62 through the town. It had been built originally as a millworker's house and now belonged to Ferranti. One of the main reasons for the move was that I should have my own room. My parents, after all, had shared with me for four years and were understandably anxious to install me somewhere else. It didn't work. The bedroom that was to have been mine was so damp as to be uninhabitable. Father got on to the Council to get something done about it, and the prevarication went on for months. Council officials would turn up, deny that there was any dampness and go away again. In the end my father saturated the walls with a wet brush, and invited the Council to take another look. They were unimpressed. We never could use that room and it remained shut off for the eight years that we lived there.

It was a tightly run household. My mother had a little tin

money box with five compartments in it – one for the rent, one for the groceries and so on. Each week she would apportion my father's paypacket carefully between them and lock the box when she had finished. The key was kept on a piece of string tied to the lid – a logic which I never did unravel.

I was twelve when Grandad generously shared his compensation money with us and we moved to our very own bungalow. I still look at it when I go back to Oldham: it's a tiny, shoe-box thing in a rather sad cul-de-sac, but at the time it was paradise.

This is not a tale of rags to riches. I never had threadbare clothes or went barefoot. There was never an Al Capone-style vow that one day I would escape from all this and make it to the top. It was a happy, secure home, conspicuous only for its ordinariness. I mention it because this was the start I was given – as neutral a set of circumstances as you could imagine. It was only after I had given my lecture on the Management of Luck to the Chemical Society that I realized the theory was the story of my life. From these beginnings I had minimized chance and maximized the chance remaining, almost by instinct, for as long as I could remember.

I was fortunate enough to be bright at school. I got eight O-levels without really trying, then promptly fell flat on my face and failed all my A-levels except Chemistry. This provoked no great surprise or outrage at home – luckily or unluckily, depending on how you look at it. My parents had approved of my going to grammar school, the first member of the family ever to do so. But the expectation was that I'd leave when I was sixteen. Passing A-levels and going to university was no part of the family consciousness. It wasn't that they couldn't afford it or didn't want to make sacrifices to pay for it: further education was outside the accepted pattern.

Imbued with this attitude, I could afford to treat my A-level years as years of privilege to use as I liked. I enjoyed Chemistry and worked at it. I also read a great deal, sat a General Studies paper, played a lot of chess and sport and ran the school debating society. With so much to keep me occupied, Maths and Physics A-levels went by the board.

Not surprisingly I fell foul of my grammar school head-master. We called him Ding-Dong, and he and I were frequently at odds. Our contretemps did wonders for my powers of awareness and judgement – not to mention my courage and flexibility. They also showed me how not to be a manager.

When I think of Ding-Dong, I picture him lining up ten seventeen-year-old lads in his study – myself among them – and saying to us, 'You know, I 'ave the power to make or break any one of you.' He meant, of course, that we wouldn't get to university without his reference. To a man, our sole concentration was on trying not to laugh, simply at the incongruity of this figure of authority dropping his 'h'. Which is ludicrous, looking back on it. This was Lancashire, the home of the dropped 'h', and we all did it all the time. But for some reason, hearing it from your own headmaster was extremely funny.

I first offended Ding-Dong when I was elected prefect against his wishes. He then took exception to my plans for a school debating society. There had been one in the school a few years previously and it had folded, so I thought I'd try and revive it. Ding-Dong began to make vague noises of disapproval. I ignored them and soldiered on. His opposition became more outspoken. The crunch came after a few successful debates when we pinned up the notice for the next meeting: 'This house deplores the existence of the masonic guilds.' He sent for me.

'That's not a suitable title, Burke.'

I thought, Click! He's a mason. All the more reason for doing it.

'What's more,' he continued. 'I forbid you to 'old the meeting.'

I realized then why the previous society had failed. It had obviously been squashed by Ding-Dong when it started debating topics he didn't like. Had he said, 'You can't debate masonic guilds because by definition you know nothing about them,' his logic would have carried weight and I would probably have conceded. But for whatever reason, he was unable to trust to logic and had to resort to an outright ban.

Things became worse when he realized I wasn't going to

university. At the time, there were only ten of us in the sixth form, so my opting out deprived him of 10 per cent of his head count.

The final confrontation arose over twenty Piccadilly cigarettes.

Every Thursday there was a divided assembly so that the headmistress could talk to the girls about sanitary towels and other mysterious womanly things (or so we always imagined) while the boys got to hear about girls and smoking and the respective dangers of each. Most weeks Green and Atkinson would be hauled on stage for smoking behind the bikesheds. 'Don't do it again,' Ding-Dong would bark. 'Filthy, 'abit ... dangerous ... stop it!' At about the same time my maths was sliding downhill. Ding-Dong – who, to give him his due, took a proper interest in his students' performance – summoned my father and told him I had to improve. My father promised to take the matter up with me.

Shortly afterwards, I was walking along the corridor to a maths lecture when Ding-Dong stopped me. 'Ah, John,' he said, 'do me a favour'. He pressed a half crown into my hand. 'Pop along to the corner and get me twenty Piccadilly.'

'No, sir, I won't,' I said.

He looked startled. 'I'm sorry?'

'Look,' I said. 'We've just come from an assembly that says, "Thou shalt not smoke." You've just had my father in here to tell him how weak I am at maths. And now, with me on my way to a maths lecture, you ask me to get you twenty Piccadilly. I'm sorry, I won't do it.'

This was not self-righteousness; nor was it any desire to humiliate my adversary. That answer was driven by awareness and judgement – awareness that Ding-Dong was hopelessly compromised; judgement that I could stand my ground as a mere sixteen-year-old and not be intimidated. What was Ding-Dong going to do? Call for my parents? Dismiss me? The *Oldham Chronicle* would have had a field day. The logic of my position – and his – was there in an instant. Being certain of my awareness and judgement, I did not even need a great deal of courage. The answer came politely and naturally: 'No.'

That episode was an important lesson. It showed me that awareness and judgement can strengthen your hand to an extraordinary degree. It was also my discovery that I could be my own man and survive. What is more, the tangle in which Ding-Dong then found himself arose from his own deficiencies in awareness, judgement, courage and flexibility. His predicament that day has been a warning to me ever since of what can happen when a manager loses hold of one or more of those four qualities.

Out from school, I followed the plan the family had mapped out and went into ICI's research division as a trainee chemist. Working in my own time and on day release, I retook maths and physics and passed them both.

ICI was an eye-opener. The place was Blackley, Manchester, down in the valley below Crumpsall. The ICI building was a vast, E-shaped edifice with hundreds of identical laboratories – a research honeycomb populated with worker bees. As one of the lowliest of those bees, I cast an eye to the top of the organization and noticed straightaway that the people with the power, the kudos and the money were PhD's. Beneath them was a phalanx of BSc's and MSc's. The lesson was clear: if you wanted to be among the decision-makers, you had to be academically well qualified. One thing I have usually managed to avoid is self-delusion (I *think* – unless I'm deluding myself) and I knew for certain I was no boffin. Even if I'd gone to university, I didn't have the cast of mind that would make it in ICI's research division.

That awareness led to the judgement that I should change my environment. And close on the heels of judgement came the need for courage and flexibility – courage to go against the lore of the family; flexibility to get up and make the move.

My father, who worked for the same company for twenty-five years, set high value on loyalty and consistency, and the family had greeted my present job with rejoicing: 'Our John's got a place at ICI … a big name … that means prospects…security.' It was not done to throw up one's new job and walk out. Although never voiced in such terms, it was made clear that I now ought to be settling down.

I might have done so – and possibly still been there – had I not become aware of something else. The revelation, if I might call it that, took place on a Friday afternoon in 1964 in one of ICI's laboratories.

My boss had gone on holiday and had left me with a list of experiments to carry out. One of these was to treat various compounds with the gas, phosgene. Phosgene is lethal at five parts per million, which is not a lot. It's also odourless, so you don't know you're dead until you hit the ground. Not surprisingly, phosgenation concentrates the mind wonderfully.

The experiment takes place in a fume cupboard with an extractor fan that creates a partial vacuum on the other side of the glass. You wish it could be minus 100 atmospheres because quite simply you're terrified. You've spent hours fitting the apparatus together and greasing the joints so theoretically it's gas-tight. Your life literally depends on it. As you turn the tap that delivers the gas to the cylinder, you can feel the sweat trickling down your back and collecting in your waistband.

Apart from racing motorbikes, I have never concentrated so hard on a single task. I have certainly never concentrated so hard for so long. A bike race is over in a few minutes, but phosgenation goes on for several hours and there's no physical outlet for the tension you feel. You can't release it by hurtling round a racetrack: as the mental pressure builds up, all you can do is keep absolutely still.

I had never before experienced this degree of alertness – nor, I think, have I done so since in quite that way. I can't help wondering whether this peculiar state of mind allowed a thought to slip through that might not otherwise have done so. As I took the experiment through its various stages I found myself thinking, 'Hang on, there's a great machine out there I know nothing about. Someone has said something to someone else, who has said to someone else, who has said to someone else, who has said to me, "Do this experiment, watch for this and that and get the following result – preferably without killing yourself." '

In other words, the commercial decisions were all being made somewhere else. Research requirements were distilled out of those decisions and passed across to the Research Division. By two steps down the chain (I must have been about five steps down) those requirements became scientific experiments with no apparent origin or consequence. No-one explained the links. The 'grown ups' worried about such things over in the other building.

So following orders, I'd take a primary aromatic amine, diazotize it, couple it (link it with other compounds), and observe the beautiful colours that resulted. Next I'd separate the compounds, purify them, and record and describe them. But to what end? I could not have told you. Now had someone told me that things that were dyed blue in those days were not dyed very well, that the dye had certain frailties and that the company that could crack the problem would make a lot of money, not just for itself but for its employees, and that one of the solutions might possibly be found in this experiment, I would have had a very different view of what I was doing.

Sweating over my fume cupboard, that day in 1964, I began to perceive that other dynamics were at work. At that point I couldn't describe them, but I knew they must exist, and I knew they must explain why I was here doing what I was doing. And I realized I would far rather be there than here.

The experience reinforced the judgement that I ought to be somewhere else. But again there were obstacles. If moving jobs was bad enough from my family's point of view, moving into a commercial job was even worse. There was not much commercial awareness at home. Father was an engineer, still at the bottom of the heap and so still seeing problems from an engineer's rather than a businessman's perspective. As a socialist and a trade unionist he was suspicious of marketing men and fancy salesmen who went to work in suits and drove flash cars. It needed courage, therefore, to fix an appointment with the Director of Personnel to talk about a change.

I knew my case was shaky. Surrounded by people with honours degrees and strings of letters after their names, who was I to be asking favours? I faced the Director of Personnel across his enormous desk and began my speech. 'I realize,' I said, 'that I'm lucky to be in the chemical industry, especially as it includes pharmaceuticals which I'm particularly interested in. And I'm lucky to be at ICI which has a pharmaceuticals division. So what I'd like to do, sir, please, is move from dyestuffs to pharmaceuticals and from research chemistry into selling, because that's where I'd rather be.'

But for whatever reason, it couldn't be done. Ironically, I had to leave ICI to join the pharmaceuticals industry.

As it happened, I did not have the courage to go oneshot into selling. My upbringing told me I didn't have the accent, the charisma, the presence for the job. Nor did I go immediately into pharmaceuticals. Instead I joined an ink manufacturer and became a technical rep.

It seemed like a smart move, for the technical rep occupies a useful intermediate position between pure selling and pure science. When the going gets rough on the technical side, you can say you're a salesman and rush back to head office for help. And vice versa.

However, I had not reckoned on my new employers' appalling record on training. Put it down to my own lack of awareness, but it made life difficult – if interesting – in the months that followed.

The phone would ring at two in the morning. I'd get out the van, already kitted up with inks and rollers, and drive across Lancashire to a printing firm in Liverpool or Wigan. There I'd be shown a five million-pound, seven-unit, photo-gravure printing machine, usually a model I'd never seen before in my life, and be told to make it go. 'Something's wrong with the ink' was the usual diagnosis. With down-time at thousands of pounds a minute I could hear the ticking in the manager's mind as I tried to sort it out. In the small hours of the morning, with sweaty palms and stark fear inside, I tackled problems I didn't understand and even solved a few. And usually it wasn't the ink at all, but the rollers, the paper, or some perversity of the union that had caused the snarl-up.

The latter could never be discounted. I knew a man who cut his finger off on a carton finisher simply to get the compensation. I've seen members of print unions altering humidity settings so it looked as though drying times would be longer and they could then negotiate higher rates. I've seen seven men operating a three-man Rotamec printer for which the management had paid £5 million, precisely so they *could* get by with three men. But in this case the Father of the Chapel had the rulebook, and the rulebook said you run photo-gravure three-colour with seven men. So seven men it was, and £5 million went down the drain.

I have asked myself since then whether my brief career in ink was bad luck or good. My conclusion is that any luck involved was purely a function of my own response. I might have decided that my family were right – that I should have stayed at ICI, where the problems were at least manageable. But to have slunk home would, I believe, have turned this episode into unadulterated bad luck. Instead, I read it as confirmation that I *did* prefer selling and ought to go all the way – not half way, as I had done so far. This decision, in turn, led to one of the best pieces of luck of my whole career.

By now I was engaged, and my future father-in-law was a pharmacist. I was able to get his perspective on the industry and to find out from him which were the companies to go for.

In due course I got a job with Beecham as a medical rep, and at the age of twenty-two left home for the first time to start my training in London. I had been to London only twice, once to the Motor Show and once when I was a child and a neighbour took me down for a treat. I remember that neighbour well. He was an interior decorator called Stuart Wallace, and he lived next door with his wife, Muriel, and a cat, Tiddles. He was an avid Manchester United supporter, drove a Norton Dominator 99 and had previously been in the army. I can still recite his army number. I wish I could forget it: it's probably taking up brain space that could more usefully be filled with something else. The fact that Stuart has so stuck in my memory must have something to do with that first trip to London and the impression it made on me as a child. Now, as a young Beecham recruit, I was on my way again to the fabled city. The world, it seemed, was opening in front of me. It was an exciting time.

I realize now that my three jobs in five years were a continuous, if subconscious, process of extending my control over circumstance; becoming aware, making decisions, stepping out. What remained, and what I could never have foreseen, was my extraordinary luck in landing at the feet of Squadron Leader O.H. Pippard.

The Beecham Training Centre at Brentford was, and still is, an organization full of dauntingly efficient people. As the most junior sprog of all, my first need was for a short, intensive period of training – and Pippard it was who trained me. Known to everyone at Beecham as Pip, Squadron Leader Pippard had served on Blenheim night fighters and had come from there into industry teaching. He was a shortish man, with twinkly eyes and a slight West Country burr. I have always admired crisp communicators, and that was the quality I first noticed in him. The man was refreshingly free of obfuscation. In many ways he was the antithesis of Ding-Dong – broad in his interests, shrewd in his judgement of people, the superlative manager. He also recognized a good piece of luck when it came his way.

During the war, his squadron had started off in short-nosed Blenheims, this being the early model with the stubby front end and the engines on the wings protruding slightly forward of the nose. The RAF then introduced a long-nosed model, filling the extra space at the front with new electrical gear. This completely altered the way the aircraft handled, especially on landing. The new model had a nasty habit of stalling on approach, and the RAF ploughed several of them into the ground. Not surprisingly, the long-nosed Blenheim got a bad reputation and the pilots in Pip's squadron were getting rebellious about flying it. He was wrestling with this man-management problem when it was solved for him by a complete stroke of luck.

Over the fence one day appeared a long-nosed Blenheim arriving from the manufacturers. It came in low over the aerodrome, climbed, rolled, looped, sat on its back and generally did all the things that a long-nosed Blenheim shouldn't. In seconds, the entire squadron was out on the apron, watching. The aircraft came in with a stick-back, flap-down roll, and just when it should have stalled it kissed the runway and rolled to a halt. The propellor stopped, the canopy slid back and a surprisingly small pilot climbed out. Off came the helmet and long, blonde hair tumbled over her shoulders. As it happened, women pilots were often used for delivery and ferry work, but none had ever arrived with quite the style of this one. From that day, there was never another grumble from the pilots. Pip no doubt wished he had thought of this stratagem himself, but had to admit it was none of his doing. All the same, he exploited it to the full to stop his pilots grumbling about the new model.

Pip was a man with his own distinct style. In the middle of the course, just six weeks before I was due to be married, my fiancée's father died. My own father telegraphed the news. 'ALEC DIED 6AM THIS MORNING STOP BODY LEEDS INFIRMARY STOP FAMILY KNOWS STOP JOHN BURKE SENIOR EN ROUTE DERBY COLLEGE STOP BACK 6.30PM STOP REGARDS.' That was typical of my father's communicating style: 'Those are the facts ... that is all you need to know ... this is what I am doing (picking up your fiancée from college) ... now be your own man and decide what you will do.'

Pip brought me the telegram in the course of the lesson. 'Sorry John,' he said. 'Bit of bad news. Here's a telegram from your father.' At the end of the lesson he asked me what I was going to do. I said I would take a stroll during the coffee break and make up my mind.

'I'm going home,' I said to him later in the morning.

Pip replied by opening his drawer and pulling out an airline ticket from Heathrow to Manchester. 'There you are,' he said. 'There's a car waiting to take you to your hotel to collect your things, and you're booked on this flight.'

There, if ever I saw it, was good management in action. Pip had made himself aware of the situation, had judged (correctly) what my response would be, had shown considerable resource in procuring a ticket while I was walking round the quadrangle, and, not least, had been brave enough to buy an air ticket on spec. Pip, like my father, was one of that enviable breed who really are their own men. His example bore out much of the philosophy I had imbibed at home.

Pip's course for reps-to-be covered not just selling skills but also physiology and anatomy – essential knowledge for anyone selling pharmaceutical products. I had never studied natural sciences in my life and some of my fellow students were biology BSc's, but such was Pip's effect on me that I came from behind to take the course prize. He didn't exactly say, 'I think you can be Chairman of Glaxo Pharmaceuticals in twenty years', but what he did do was lift my psychological ceiling and give me confidence in my own abilities.

Subconsciously, perhaps, I was still oppressed by the fact that I wasn't a graduate. To that point I had tended to think that knowledge was paramount: if you had it, you could do anything; if you hadn't, you were disadvantaged. Though I wouldn't have expressed it in quite these terms, I was stuck with a linear view of awareness, judgement, courage and flexibility. I felt that until you were fully equipped with the first, you couldn't move on to acquire the others. I now think differently. As we'll see later on, the four are integrated one with another and need not be sequential. How aware you become, for instance, is often a function of how flexible or brave you are prepared to be.

Pip, wisely, did not see my lack of knowledge as an obstacle to progress, and succeeded in motivating me as nobody had ever done before. For the first time off the race track, I felt competitive. It was as though my pores had opened and I could soak in everything I was offered. I have never worked so hard in my life, and the harder I worked, as though by alchemy, the more luck materialized. Paradoxically, the realization that lack of knowledge was not an obstacle made me hungrier for it, and I couldn't get enough of it.

The death of my fiancée's father interrupted the eight-week course by a week, so when I came back I had a lot of catching up to do. By then we had dealt with the major products and were on to the tail-enders. Pip suggested I skip them, but I wouldn't have it. I crammed in every detail of every single product until in the end I was the only man there who could reel off the details of Ferroplex B, the twenty-seventh product on our list and the one that everyone else was forgetting.

Other than my father, no-one has done more for me as an individual than O.H. Pippard in the eight short weeks of that course.

In one sense, the salesman is the most powerless of people, constantly at the beck and call of his customers. In another, he exercises extraordinary power. As a Pippard-trained medical rep of twenty-two, I would call on Professors of Cardiology and influence them as to which drugs they should be using. Working now, not on chemical compounds but on people. I came to realize that you cannot manage a business unless you are steeped in how people work.

In short, I began to understand the psychological skills that a manager needs to acquire.

CHAPTER FIVE

Foibles and Absurdities: How To Become Aware

THE MORE you understand the events taking place around you, the better equipped you will be to extend your control over chance. So rule one in the management of luck is to become as aware as you possibly can.

The starting point is the straightforward gathering of data. If you're launching a new product, you'll obviously look at the market dynamics. Who's in there? What is the shape and size of the competition? What are the relative market shares? How long have your competitors been there? What is the patent situation? And so on. Every manager does it, well or badly depending on his own data-gathering skills and the quality of his support.

Observing two simple rules will help.

One: make it clear that you yourself actually *want* to know the facts. 'No surprises,' my one-time American boss used to say. 'Tell me the good news, tell me the bad, tell it all and tell it thoroughly. The one thing I will not forgive is that by keeping news to yourself I hear it from someone I should not hear it from, and I'm unprepared.'

Two: to avoid being inundated, brief your staff on the quality and quantity of information you need. Churchill's famous memo is an excellent model: 'Pray inform me this day on one sheet of paper the state of His Majesty's Navy.'

Not only must you have the data; you must also know what the data means[1].

First impressions can be misleading. To take facts simply at face value can blind you to both the dangers and the opportunities they contain. Take the case of a government ban on a particular chemical that appears in your product. Good luck or bad luck? It sounds like bad luck, but you won't know for sure unless you investigate and push your awareness a little further.

When my own company faced this situation a few years ago, I found that a little time spent analyzing the effect on my competitors as well as on myself produced some interesting conclusions.

Take the following market analysis:

Total market value	100
Market value of your product A	30
Market value of your product B	10
Competitors' market value	60
	100

Let us now assume the following:

Your product B and two thirds of the competitor market contain the banned compound.

All products can compete in all markets.

The market remains at 100.

You take market share from the banned products proportionate to your present market share with product A.

The equation now looks like this:

Total market value	100
Market value of your product A	45
Market value of your product B (now banned)	0
Competitors' market value	55
	100

---

[1] Yes, I know data are plural, but the plural usage now sounds so odd I'm going to keep them singular.

The result of the ban is an increase of five percentage points in your own market share – from 40 to 45 per cent. But you might argue that your own pick-up will be proportionate to your total market share as a company, not just the share enjoyed by product A. This alters the equation again:

Total market value	100
Market value of your product A	50
Market value of your product B (now banned)	0
Competitors' market value	50
	100

Your market value has now grown from 40 to 50 per cent. You can even change some assumptions for the worse and still enjoy 'good luck'. For example, the market might shrink by as much as 20 per cent as a result of the ban, but if you simply retain your new share you will still equal your original 40 per cent of market by value.

Awareness, then, should cover not just the facts but what the facts imply for your company.

If data existed in some pure form, and all we had to do was pick it like apples from a tree, awareness would be easy to come by. As always, life is never quite that simple. All facts, other than those which your own experience confirms, reach you through the mediation of other people. In gathering information, you must therefore take account of the individuals you are getting it from. Which means understanding how people work.

Here, in my view, is the single most important ingredient in successful management. The clean, logical, Swiss watch-type of company does not exist. It is people who make a business, and people have vague, messy edges to them. I would not have it otherwise, but it means the corporate jigsaw will never be a perfect fit. You have to make adjustments. In the end, you're dealing with people and their frailties, and you stand or fall as a manager by how well you accommodate them.

As we've already seen, 'chance' is often nothing more than the consequence of human actions. To extend his control over chance, therefore, the good manager must aspire to be a practising psychologist.

People in general spend a great deal of time thinking about circumstances, but very little time considering the psychologies of the individual men and women who have made those circumstances what they are. Although I know relatively little of psychological theory, I have tried as a manager to give attention to this neglected side of the equation. After all, management consists of little other than understanding people and communicating with them. Because information is mediated by people, it can come distorted in a variety of ways depending on who supplies it.

I recall how on one occasion a pharmaceutical development conceived by the marketing department had a rough ride at the hands of the company's scientists, who were no doubt miffed that they hadn't thought of it first. The scientists carried out the early clinical trials and presented their results: 'Patients taking the drug showed no significant improvement over those who took a placebo.'

We dug a little deeper. The numerical version of that summary read thus: 'Only 7 per cent improvement between active and placebo: not statistically significant.' Getting down to the actual figures, we discovered that 17 per cent of patients given the placebo got better, while 24 per cent of patients on the new compound improved. The difference was not 7 per cent, but 7 on 17 which is 41 per cent and highly significant. The 'Not Invented Here' syndrome had struck again and had nearly prevented a useful new drug coming to market.

So some people will fail to give you the facts for purposes of their own. All too often, it seems, the enemies of accurate awareness are within your own company. Others will give you the wrong facts because they do not know the right ones and will not admit it. Some will present the right facts, beautifully tooled to make you receive them one way or another.

But it isn't always somebody else's mischief or ignorance that causes the trouble. In my experience, one of the greatest obstacles to true information is self-delusion. I have worked in at least one company with a sparkling record of innovative products, the kind of company that is so successful it seems impossible for management to put a foot wrong. Insidiously, the prevailing attitude becomes: 'We're successful, so everything we do must be right. We have the right management structure, the right selection procedure, the right training programmes,' and so on. This is a difficult habit to break. It takes real courage to say to a man who has taken the company from X to 50X in ten years, 'Are you sure?' But unless that question is constantly voiced, perception will start straying from reality.

A doctor can look at people and know things about them that a layman would not, simply with the knowledge he has of disease and the ageing process and the way they manifest themselves. In the same way, the good manager will read the psychological condition of his colleagues and staff. Begin to do so, and you will find people behaving in the most extraordinary ways – ways which have nothing to do with logic or good business practice, but which more often reflect deep-seated needs in the individuals themselves.

When a company's fleet of chauffeur-driven cars is not sufficient to meet demand, it is sometimes necessary to bring in hire cars from outside. On several occasions when that has happened, I have seen the most intense rivalry between directors as to who took company cars and who had to make do with rented cars. The cars themselves were identical, but the rented versions were definitely regarded as inferior. It doesn't take much to expose the insecurities of even the most competent individuals.

But the reasons for odd behaviour can be far more complex than simple status-seeking. I had a boss at Searle called Anatole Schwieger. He was Polish, a Jew, and the most cosmopolitan man I have ever met. He grew up speaking not only Polish but Ukrainian. When the Germans swept into Poland during World War II, he learned German. When the Russians swept in, he learned Russian. When the war was over, he went to the USA and learned English. He finished his education in France, so learned French. His first management job was in Holland, so he learned Dutch. By the time I knew him he had roughly a dozen languages at his command and could speak like a native in all of them. And he absorbed not just languages but cultures. From heraldry to rose-growing, from wines to politics, Anatole Schwieger could set out an argument and support it at a moment's notice in whatever language you chose.

He took over the European presidency of Searle UK from an ex-British Army colonel who as late as 1978 had still not led Searle in any serious way into the markets of Germany or Japan, despite the fact that these two countries are the second and third largest pharmaceutical markets in the world.

Anatole, who'd had a far worse war than his predecessor (he'd actually spent some years in a concentration camp) bore none of the bitterness you might have expected. Mercurial, temperamental, frenetic, this firework of a man fizzed around the globe, building his empire and generally being uncomfortable to live with. I owe him an enormous debt for knocking my parochialism out of me, putting me on aeroplanes and shooting me off around the world, but for all that, our personalities never quite sat comfortably together. He, Mr Cosmopolitan, living chaotically on his instincts; me, the boy from Oldham, phlegmatic and linear-thinking as the English tend to be. Indeed, our first meeting could well have been our last.

He was interviewing me for the job of Marketing Director in Searle UK. He shot out his list of questions and appeared satisfied. Then he asked if I had any questions to put to him.

'Oh yes,' I replied, pulling my list from my pocket. It was a long list and I started working through it. Suddenly Anatole looked at his watch.

'My God, is that the time? Do you realize you've kept me? I've got a plane to catch to Switzerland.' And he got up to go.

It was Ding-Dong and the twenty Piccadilly all over again. Knowing I had right on my side, I decided not to let him get away with it. 'Mr Schwieger,' I said, 'you never asked whether I've got a plane too. Quite rightly you've had the first chunk of this conversation, but I understood that I would have a similar claim on your time. This is a big move for me. It's important I have some questions answered. Shall we meet some other time?'

He relented. I got my questions answered and in due course came over from Beecham to take the job.

In time, I got used to Anatole's energetic way of doing things, and to the paternalism he showed to his senior managers.

Anatole was exceptional in this regard, not for his paternalism, but for the fact that he knew he practised it, for most people are unaware of the internal needs they're trying to feed. Take the case of the manager who accepts the ideas of his staff and passes them on without tampering with them. He then defends those ideas to the death – and often it *is* to the death because he hasn't thought them out and they don't work. So he comes back and says, 'Sorry lads, the bosses won't implement it.' The staff in turn think, 'He's a good sort. At least he listens. It's the idiots upstairs who can't see the wood for trees.' What this manager has done is defend people's ideas because he wants their affection, even if the ideas themselves are rotten. In so doing he does everyone a disservice – himself, the so-called idiots upstairs and his staff, because they now become jaundiced in a way that is inappropriate and unrelated to the facts. If he *is* feeding his internal needs, the least he can do is acknowledge the fact, so that innocent parties don't get blamed. But if he doesn't know he's doing it, he can't acknowledge it, and so the poison spreads.

In one of my companies I once carried out a test to see how impartially a cross-section of international MDs could report on their own markets. Over cocktails in a London hotel, the evening before we all met for a conference, I asked fifty or sixty individuals from all over the world what market share they had achieved with a given product. White men, black men, yellow men, brown men all gave the answer in cash, not volume.

'Sixty per cent,' they'd say, sipping at the Bloody Mary.

'That must be in cash.'

'Yes.'

'What is it in volume?' I would ask.

At least a dozen of my respondents didn't know. A similar number said they couldn't tell me but thought it was higher than the competitor's share. The conclusion I drew was that all my respondents instinctively gave the figure that made them look good. What's more, they didn't realize they were doing it, because none of them was at all embarrassed by my supplementary question. The danger was, however, that by looking at their businesses in cash rather than in volume terms, they were drawing a wrong conclusion as to what had been achieved, and would therefore have a wrong picture of what was left to achieve. Concern to preserve the ego had muddied awareness, which in turn would impair judgement. My quest to measure the pragmatism of my colleagues had uncovered an alarming degree of self-delusion.

The good manager sees things as they really are, and that means being free of awkward, distorting internal needs. (I think I hear Kipling rustling in the background.) But which of us can claim that happy state? We're human, after all. Let me rephrase the point and say that proper awareness requires knowledge of other people's obfuscating tendencies, plus, most importantly, an appreciation of your own. If you understand the psychological mechanisms at work, and are able then to compensate, you're a long way towards accurate perception.

This principle, which I practised unknowingly for years, was formally expressed for me only when I attended a course at the Levinson Institute in Boston. It was Anatole who sent me, possibly thinking that this lad from Oldham needed a little more managerial finesse than he had so far exhibited.

The Levinson Institute specializes in some of the psychological aspects of management, and there I first encountered the formula,

$$SE = \frac{1}{EI - SI}$$

where SE stands for self-esteem, EI for ego-ideal and SI for self-image. Self-esteem, in other words, is the reciprocal of your ego-ideal minus your self-image. So the further your self-image is from your ego-ideal, the smaller the right hand side of the equation and the lower your self-esteem. The young Winston Churchill was a classic sufferer. Old Sir Randolph set such impossibly high standards that his son – stammering, not very bright at school and not very strong physically – found his self-image trailing behind the ideal. Consequently, his own self-esteem was very low. He was not unusual. Most people would like their self-esteem to be higher, so devote much of their energy to dragging their self-image up to their ego ideal.

In other words, if you look better expressing your market performance in cash rather than in volume, that is what you will do, and never mind if it blurs the facts and distorts your subsequent judgement.

Pippard was a contrary case. For whatever reason, his self-image was sufficiently close to his ego-ideal for him not to have to feed off me – or anyone else for that matter. Perhaps that is why he came across so clearly as his own man; as someone who had no need to obfuscate. The good practising psychologist, the one who sees things as they really are, is, by and large, the whole man or woman. It's the unwhole man or woman with the psychological gap who is dangerous. The person who needs friendship or power or respect to close the gap in his psyche will not see the facts, will not judge rightly, and will inflict a distorted, damaging style of management on those around him.

And the gap can reveal itself in surprising ways. Sexual harassment, for example, is one of its more bizarre symptoms. Normally, when it's spotted, people hope it will go away. At most, someone has a quiet word with the culprit and asks him not to do it again. The assumption is that sexual harassment is a private problem, unrelated to a man's performance as a manager. Not so. The man who is sexually harassing his colleagues may well be covering up his deficient self-esteem in other ways as well. True awareness will mean reinterpreting his actions with that knowledge in mind.

So in making yourself aware, you've gathered your data and you've read the psychologies of those around you. It is then a good idea to avoid categorizing this information for as long as you can. I find for myself that I'm gleaning information all the time – sucking it up like a vacuum cleaner – subconsciously as much as consciously. But I try not to compartmentalize it. Obviously I need some mental filing system or I couldn't handle it, but I've found enormous benefit in letting the facts rattle around in my head until something turns the key and they fall into place.

Very often that something is an additional psychological perception. Many a time I've been given information about a person – 'You must meet X, he's like this, done that, been there,' – and I've held it all in limbo while looking out for the key that explains the man. Sometimes it's the kind of car he drives, sometimes the way he dresses, sometimes his body language. Any of these is capable of interpreting and reordering the data people have given me.

So cruise around the problem. Search out the peripheral data, especially the psychological data, for you're not dealing with 'The Marketing Manager' or 'The Director of Research', you're dealing with human beings, and you have to take account of all the foibles and absurdities of human beings. If you can discern their internal dynamics through the clues they give, your awareness will be that much more complete.

I was once waiting to be appointed to a company board, and my colleagues were showing keen interest in when the invitation would come. For all sorts of good business reasons, it would sensibly have fallen in a particular month, and that was when most people in the company expected it. I was alone in insisting that it would actually happen some months later. My colleagues thought I must have inside information, which was not the case and I said so.

'I have the same information as you,' I insisted, 'but I'm trying to look at the psychological aspects of the case as well.'

Pressed to explain what I had deduced and they had not, I

wrote down the vital information on a card, sealed it in an envelope and gave it to someone to keep. The earlier date came and went and the appointment failed to materialize. Then my date came and it happened. The envelope was opened. Written on the card was the date of the Chairman's birthday. He had been the youngest ever member of the board when he was first appointed – a fact which all of us knew full well. But had he brought me in on the earlier date, I would have pipped his record and he certainly wasn't having that. As it was, I joined the board just late enough for him to keep his record.

There's no black art here. I don't have a goa[...] Peter Sellers Austrian accent. I'm simply a wo[...] who spends as much time studying the psycho[...] of a problem as the more traditional aspects. B[...] to awareness, and I try to evaluate them both.

My lifelong interest in foibles and absurditi[...] me again and again into contact with 'The Pact'[...] mentality is the enemy of being your own[...] mentality is the enemy of proper awareness.[...] enemy of judgement, courage and flexibility, [...] to these in later chapters.)

By pact mentality, I mean mutual cover-up[...] question or raise this, I won't question or r[...] biggest culprits in my experience are a[...] managers. Like penguins, we all turn up to th[...] walk round in circles to keep each other warr[...] anything about exports,' we chant. 'The poun[...] We can then all report back to our respect[...] everyone is in the same boat.

'Sorry, sir, but it's all the fault of the pound.[...]

'Are you sure?'

'Absolutely. I was down at this meeting [...] from motor manufacturing to coal mining it's the same story.'

The trouble is, when the currency situation reverses, there's a new crop of excuses as to why some companies are not performing as well as they might. Like the emperor's new clothes, the pretence relies on everyone sticking to the story,

Erratum

With apologies to the Chairman of the Committee for the Safety of Medicines, the correct spelling of whose name is Bill Asscher.

whatever the story of the day might be.

I've seen this very scenario played out at meetings of the CBI. (I don't pick specifically on the CBI; it could have happened in a dozen different contexts.) In January 1981 when the dollar stood at 2.40 to the pound, I went to a CBI meeting and the talk was all about the strength of sterling and how difficult it was to export as a result. I remember thinking at the time that as soon as the currency situation reversed itself, a new excuse would rise to the surface. And I wasn't disappointed. By September of the same year, the dollar had gone to 1.78. I turned up to another CBI meeting and sure enough they were all blaming the high rate of National Insurance for holding them back.

At the time, I was working for an American company and reported to Chicago in dollars. At the start of the year I would commit myself to X million dollars profit at the year-end, and regardless of currency fluctuations I was expected to meet the figure. To say to my colleagues, 'As luck would have it, Gentlemen, the currency turned against me,' would have simply brought the arm round the shoulder and the classic question, 'How long have you been with us now, John?'

In reality the comment was, 'Sure John, this is real tough. What are you going to do about it?' In other words, it is my responsibility in those circumstances to make up the difference. I cannot influence exchange rates, so I must sell more product, or effect more savings, or be more creative or efficient, or all of those things. The choice is mine, but the onus is on me to do something.

In my other favourite example of the pact the truth was trampled on, not because of any attempt to conceal it, but because all the players were locked into roles defined for them by long familiarity.

The Vice-President, who was chairing this particular meeting, had a strongly defined self-image. He saw himself – correctly, I might add – as the punchy, staccato chief executive, clearing away the brushwood with a few vigorous strokes to reveal the answer before our very eyes. His sharp style encouraged his managers to deliver crisp, decisive pronouncements from the point of view of their own disciplines. So the finance man threw in the numbers when the spotlight landed on him; the medic was ready on cue with the scientific data; and so on. The pact held sway. Meetings were like performances of a well-rehearsed play. Though the Vice-President deserved better, the participants had worked together for so long, their personal psychologies had shuffled down like a bean bag until everyone was comfortable with his part.

The issue under discussion was a regulatory threat to one of our products. Apparently someone had pointed out that its microbiological count was too high. What were we to do? Quick as a flash, the Technical Director had his answer: a variety of radiations would lower the count. What would it cost? The Financial Director threw in the figure. Marketing implications? The answer was ready. Zap, zap, zap around the table. The scene ran like a Hollywood movie – punchy chief executive has his people in place, rips from one to the next, and in minutes carves out the solution. 'OK,' he said at length, 'we'll do it.'

Until that point I hadn't spoken. The Vice-President looked up and saw me at the end of the table. I've got an unfortunate face, as my friends have often told me: it's mobility shows when my feelings are screwed up. 'What's the matter with your face, John?' he asked.

I replied with some hesitation. 'I don't think this answer makes a lot of sense.'

The pact was horrified. The Technical Director had pronounced. The answer was obvious and everyone had agreed.

'What's your problem, John?'

I said I would want to ask five questions before I assented to the proposal. I could see the Vice-President deliberating whether or not to break the mould. To his credit, he decided he would.

'What would the five questions be?'

'One,' I said. 'Who says?'

'Who says what?'

'Who says the microbiological content is too high?'

The question was fielded by the Medical Director. He gave a name. It turned out to be our competitor!

The Vice-President moved into top gear. He was going to have this rat out and nothing was going to stop him. 'What's the second question?'

'Which micro-organisms?' I continued.

Back to the Medical Director, who replied that he didn't know. I observed that this product was destined for the human bowel, which already has a hundred thousand micro-organisms per square millimetre, and that without those micro-organisms you would die.

'Third question?'

I said it was irrelevant, given the answers we'd already heard. With one or two bricks pulled from the bottom, the edifice had collapsed. There was nothing wrong with the technical solution that had been proposed: it would certainly have answered the problem which had been identified. The trouble was, this was not the problem. Microbiological counts had nothing to do with it: far more to the point were the machinations of our competitors. But no-one had seen that fact because they all were so comfortable in their roles that they had forgotten how to step out and raise an awkward question. It wasn't lack of courage that prevented my colleagues speaking up, just plain, simple lack of awareness.

The pact might be defined as a mutual attempt to smother the truth. It can happen consciously, as when penguins close ranks around an excuse, or unconsciously, when managers lapse into role-play in response to a dominant personality. Becoming aware means pact-shooting wherever possible. More practically, it means changing the corporate environment so that pacts can no longer flourish. Pacts are a survival mechanism. They imply a threat. 'If I step out of the circle, my mistakes will be exposed ... If I ask the real question, my boss will read it as impertinence.' The more you as a manager can remove this type of threat from your organization, the clearer will be your view of the truth.

Awareness, of course, should not be exclusive to management. The most successful businesses are often those in which awareness is disseminated throughout the organization. To achieve this end, I offer three management principles that I have found invaluable.

1. Present well, and help others to present well.

In every company, people are constantly communicating data to other people to make them aware and to help them make judgements. It is therefore essential to create an environment in which information flows freely. Not only must all the relevant information be present, but it has to be assembled in a way that minimizes the possibility of error.

I have chaired meetings where the file of preliminary information, handed out the evening before, was an inch thick with ins and outs and pros and cons related to the subject. Which simply does not help. The database has been too big, too cumbersome, too distracting to be useful. In short, it has not been properly presented for the purpose in hand.

Information needs to come not only in the right form, but also at the right time. I once witnessed a corporate planning process of such size and complexity that the plan itself could not be completed before the fiscal year to which it related actually began. New information, usually standard costs from the company's factories, continued to arrive well into the year in question. As this was inserted, other elements in the plan were juggled and smoothed to make it all consistent. The plan was finally completed about half way through the year – and immediately binned. Not only was it far too late to be helpful, it was actually wrong: funds that might have been available for this particular subsidiary had now been reallocated to other companies in the group. The planning process had consumed the energies of the company, but the plan itself, when completed, had no meaning. Data too late can be worse than no data at all.

My interest in proper presentation goes right back to schooldays when I saw children getting deeper and deeper into trouble, not for what they had done or not done, but because they didn't have the fluency to explain what was going on. I can picture one such child now – nit-ridden, stammering, smelling of urine – always getting picked on because he was odd and therefore a target. Having become a target – for teachers, other children, the nit-nurse – he could never assemble an argument to get himself out of trouble.

For better or worse, I have learned that good presentation usually carries you further than good substance. I have frequently seen poor thinking accepted because it was well crafted and delivered. Rarely, however, have I seen right substance overcome wrong approach. I have seen tall men talking to short men and not being heard because the height difference created such discomfort as to kill the message. Just once or twice in my management career, I have made the effort to sit with a thoroughly objectionable character because I felt he had something worth saying. In each case, when it finally came, it was a gem. But the point is, I have not done it often nor done it easily.

Becoming aware includes learning the difference between presentation and substance; it means discerning when good presentation conceals bad substance, and vice-versa. And the quest to make other people aware means harnessing the two. When I confronted Ding-Dong over his twenty Piccadilly, I knew I was right – but I was also extremely polite. Being polite *and* right is a potent combination.

2. Give people co-ordinates.

Sometimes because of the dehumanizing or trivial nature of a job and more often because of lack of management application, employees are not well informed about their companies. I have tried not to perpetuate this mistake in my companies. At every opportunity, I aim to make people aware of how their own jobs affect the business. If I say to someone on a bench, 'What are you doing?' and he replies, 'I'm diazotizing this to couple it with that,' I tend to ask why. If he doesn't know, I pursue it with his boss until I begin to recognize the underlying business plan. I'll then go back to the bench and say, 'What do you know about renal artery stenosis?' If the answer is, 'Nothing,' I'll explain that renal artery stenosis is a problem that affects the kidney, that the existing treatment has this or that drawback, and that these compounds on the bench may be part of the solution.

The co-ordinates you give need to be financial as well as technical. Where companies take the trouble to communicate their results right down to the shop floor, the exercise is generally well received.

I concede you have to be appropriate; to give people co-ordinates, whether technical or financial, that are relevant to their own place in the enterprise. There may be no point giving grandiose frames of reference to a widget-stamper who neither knows nor cares where his widgets are going. But in this case you need to provide a reduced frame of reference – something, at least, that makes him a person rather than a function.

People who have co-ordinates will do their jobs with greater awareness. If judgement is part of the job, greater awareness will make it sharper. Seeing the overall picture also gives people greater courage when they have to overcome obstacles. Finally, it makes them more flexible. It is people without co-ordinates who seek security in pacts and unions, with the loss of flexibility that that implies.

3. Encourage psychological awareness in others.

A competent negotiator will turn up to a meeting having done his sums and having at his fingertips all the data he is likely to need on markets, margins, costs and so on. But surprisingly, many negotiators go into action without doing any homework on the other party's psychology. Negligence on this score is as culpable, in my view, as failing to do the necessary mathematical calculations. I would even say that the numbers on the charts are secondary to a sound psychological assessment of the other people involved.

As I write, one of my directors is about to negotiate

business with people he has never met. The plan is this. Before that meeting, I shall be seeing those same people on another matter. I know them pretty well. My director will come with me and use the meeting to get his psychological bearings. He'll ask a few questions so he doesn't look a dummy, but all the time he'll be sizing up the style, the codes, the body language of the opposition. When he comes to his own negotiations, he'll be that much better equipped to play the factual cards in his hand. He'll know how much courage he can deploy before courage becomes foolhardiness. He'll know how flexible he can be before the other side becomes uncomfortable. In brief, his awareness will reduce the chance element of the meeting and give him greater control over its outcome.

CHAPTER SIX

Judging It Rightly

AWARENESS ON its own will not help you extend your
control over luck. It needs to be coupled with right
judgement – right judgement as to what the information
means, then right judgement as to what you must do to
extend your control over chance and make the most of the
chance that remains.

Awareness and judgement hang together. If you find
you've judged something wrongly, the fault may not be in the
judgement at all – rather in the data. So in judging, be sure
your facts are right.

In 1967, an Argonaut passenger plane on approach to
Manchester Airport began to lose power. It was an elderly,
piston-engined aircraft whose power-to-weight ratio was
notoriously low, particularly when the plane was heavily
loaded as this one was. Aware that one of his engines had
failed, the pilot decided to feather the propellor on the failed
motor to reduce the drag on the aircraft. He glanced at the
four feathering dials, reached up and made the necessary
adjustment.

The plane crashed and some of the passengers were killed.
To start with, everybody assumed it was pilot error. It was
only months later that examination of the aircraft showed that

complexities associated with the fuel feed cocks would make determination of which engine was at fault and its correction difficult.

Garbage in, garbage out: if the information is wrong and you don't know it, no amount of good judgement will produce the right solution.

But mistakes can just as easily occur, and perhaps more often do, through faulty judgement based on facts which are correct. So what makes good judgement, and how do we acquire it?

The first principle of judgement is to know how much information is appropriate. As a general rule, accumulate as much awareness as you can, for the more awareness you have, the less you leave to chance when it comes to judgement. That said, don't go looking for information after it has ceased to be useful. In my management life I have seen both extremes at work.

Some people take the gathering of data to the nth degree, going on until they have data hanging from their ears. Only as a last resort do they trust to instinct. That's because they place high value on the objective and fight shy of the subjective or intuitive. Others go to the opposite extreme, being more disposed to make judgements prematurely, *before* the right amount of data has been assembled.

Others will prolong the data-gathering process for different reasons – not because they value the information but because it avoids having to make a decision. They may be ditherers by nature. They may be unwilling to face the crunch. But few people will say, 'I'm indecisive ... I'm a coward.' Instead they will scribble across the memo, 'More clarification, please, on Item 8,' and recycle it. This, of course, is classic pact behaviour. If the pact is well entrenched, paperwork can circulate indefinitely, gathering data like barnacles until it sinks under its own weight or simply becomes irrelevant with the passage of time. Then all can breathe a sigh of relief at one more decision that did not have to be made. The pact, in this instance, has saved itself the discomfort of thinking or acting:

what it has not done is manage its luck.

Someone else who tends to gather too much data is the manager who knows that the information he is accumulating is not what he wants, but he cannot do other than ask for it – either because of his own inflexibility, or because his support systems are geared in a particular way.

In my own industry, there is a phenomenon called parallel importation: if your prices in one country rise, products will be imported at a lower price from a neighbouring country and you'll lose business. When a company faces this possibility, the instinctive reaction is to find out the level of parallel importation and then to decide what to do about it. On occasion, I have found myself speaking to one of my colleagues, deputed by the board to produce a figure. A typical exchange runs something like this:

'John, I need to know the level of parallel importation for your territory.'

'Sorry, Ken, I can't give it to you.'

'Why not?'

'Because I don't know it. Nobody knows it.'

'Well, we want your judgement.'

'OK,' I'll reply. '7 per cent.'

'Fine. When are you going to do the exercise?'

'What exercise, Ken? There's no exercise to do. I've given you my best guess of 7 per cent. I can go away, I can put a team on it, they can come back in three weeks' time and it will still be 7 per cent. It's an illusion to think you can get any closer by mathematical means because the information doesn't exist.'

'Well, that isn't good enough for me,' comes the response. 'I'll feel foolish going back to the board and saying, "Everyone's given their guesses and here is the aggregate figure." ' To which the reply has to be, 'Foolish or not, that's the position you're in.'

This response is not as dismissive as it might sound. Given the circumstances, what the board needs is not a figure to the fourth decimal point, but simply an indication of whether the threat is large or small – in other words, more costly or less costly than the necessary remedial action. That indication is usually available from existing data, but only if you're flexible (and perhaps also brave) in approaching the data in an unconventional way. So don't let your data-gathering routines blinker you to the kind of information you really need. A great deal of time and effort is wasted gathering information uselessly.

Assuming, then, that your information is sound, of the right sort and gathered in the right quantity, how do you set about judging it?

Good judgement may or may not come easily to you. You may feel it's inborn, and to some extent that is perhaps the case. But not wholly so. Judgement is a process, not a mystery, and as such can be learnt. There are steps to go through. People have written about the subject and books are available. Don't simply throw your hands in the air if you lack the necessary qualities. Go out and get them. If you need a place to start, I'd suggest Keith Jackson's excellent book, *The Art of Solving Problems*.[1]

For my part, I offer these five steps to good judgement.

1. Identify the problem you're trying to solve.

You have your data before you, and for some reason you're sitting in judgement on it. Unless it's for fun – like a crossword puzzle – you have an end in view as you enter the process. It's essential to define that end, and surprisingly easy not to do so.

I have met people in both my business and my personal life who are profoundly worried by the problems that beset them. You ask what the matter is, and the answer, frequently, is an outpouring of how horrible it all is rather than a description of the problem. If you identify and understand the problem, you will then know what must happen for the problem no

---

[1] Available from Dr K.F. Jackson (publisher), The Rowans, Marsham Way, Gerrards Cross, Bucks SL9 8AD.

longer to be a problem, which sets you off immediately on the road to finding a solution. But until that point you are paralysed. As the Cheshire Cat observed to Alice, if you don't know where you want to get to, it doesn't matter which way you go.

2. Weigh the data.

If judgement were a formula, and all you had to do was feed in facts at one end and see what popped out at the other, we would all be top-class managers. In reality, all information must be weighed before it can be used, for you need to know the value to put upon it. While there is no substitute here for experience, one or two techniques can keep you from obvious blunders.

One is to play the record backwards and look for the absurdity which wrong weighting has built in. I recall one marketing meeting where an entire team became tremendously excited about a product's potential, saw that the chairman was excited, and to avoid breaking ranks with the pact became more excited still. As we worked on the figures, our possible market share grew larger and larger until we were throwing our hats in the air with jubilation. Then somebody said, 'Hang on … we've just described a market share for this drug that is twice the number of available patients.' Something, somewhere, had been wrongly weighted. It needed a view from the other end – a look at the implications in another part of the forest – for the error to be exposed.

A second precaution against wrong weighting is to know your own level of optimism or pessimism. If you're over-optimistic, you will probably not have challenged the data sufficiently. If your problem is pessimism, you'll never move forward because you'll spend your time cross-checking in circles. The question is, how do you know which way you tend? Fortunately you can find out, through the new and extremely useful technique of psychometry. We'll look at this in more detail in the next chapter.

3. *Leave the obstacles until the end.*

You have defined your objectives; you have given appropriate weight to all your data; now you're looking for ways of solving the problem. It's at this point that obstacles can rear their heads and become all-absorbing. You ask for solutions and people say very quickly, 'We could do this, except that …' I have learned over the years to forbid this knee-jerk reaction.

My technique now is to set out all the possibilities, including the most outrageous, and to start choosing between them only when the full list is on the table. That is the point at which to address the obstacles and decide whether or not they can be overcome. The problem with dismissing options at the start is that variations on those ideas – variations that might in fact be feasible – are lost to you forever.

Jackson in his book rules out the term, 'problem-solving', calling it instead, 'result-getting'. 'Problem-solving' fixes the eye on the wrong place. It puts the obstacles at the beginning and can make them unnecessarily frightening.

I myself try to start from the position that there is no problem. If I simply ask, 'What needs to have happened for this problem no longer to be a problem?' the answer is frequently, 'Very little'. Problems, like good and bad luck, have a way of turning inside out. A slight shift of perspective can transform obstacle into opportunity – and interestingly, the size is retained. It seems almost a natural law that the greater the adversity, the greater the benefit if you can swing it 180 degrees. Ask Norman Croucher. Ask Solzhenitsyn.

A shoe manufacturer, so the well-known story goes, sent two representatives to open up a new market in a primitive corner of Africa. The first cabled back, 'No opportunity here … nobody wears shoes.' The message from the second ran thus: 'Amazing opportunity … nobody wears shoes.'

Nothing impairs judgement as much as preoccupation with the problems. Pushing the problems to the back of the queue at least gives time for those that are spurious to collapse.

4. *Do not let the plan restrict the aspiration.*

The process of judgement falls into stages. Having gathered the facts, you must evaluate them; having evaluated, you must plan; having planned, you must implement.

We have looked already at the first of those transitions and noted the dangers of gathering too much or too little data before you start evaluating. The second transition – from evaluation to planning – presents dangers of its own, especially if you leave out that important ingredient, aspiration.

The line of least resistance when you're planning is to set up a forecast that will probably happen anyway – to say, 'Here is our market ... here is our market share ... here is our historical performance projected out ... therefore here is our plan.' The pact loves this approach: it represents the least possible risk and allows you to state your figures with resounding conviction. You know the pact has been at work when growth projections are given to the nearest tenth of a percentage point.

But this is cart before the horse – the aspiration determined by the plan, which in turn is determined by past performance. Where is the opportunity here for minimizing chance and maximizing the chance remaining? It is far more constructive – if uncomfortable – to fix the aspiration first and mould the plan to it.

When presented with a pact-type plan, I have sometimes made the comment, 'Wouldn't you like twice that figure on the bottom line?'

'Of course we would,' they say, looking at me as though I were mad.

'Well, why don't you do it?'

The answer is, either they haven't thought of it or they haven't thought it was possible. So we clear the decks and run through a sequence something like this.

'Take ten out of the bottom and write twenty,' I begin. 'Let's consider now what we must do to make that happen.'

The easiest answer is to change the assumptions on which

the plan is based – to state, for example, that the market will expand at twice the rate. But that's fantasy, not reality. If you're going to have to *do* things to make it twenty and not ten, instantly there are all the reasons in the world as to why it's not possible.

'It'll need enormous promotional power,' says the pact.

'Can we afford it?'

'Yes, we can afford it, but we'll have to double the number of reps.'

'Are they available?'

'Oh, yes.'

'Well, why don't you hire them?'

'Because they won't be as good as our people.'

'How do you know?'

'It stands to reason. They don't belong. They have no team spirit, no dedication.'

'They might if you convinced them of the product.'

The pact shifts its ground. 'Well, our own people would feel offended if a whole lot of strangers came in and started selling their product.'

'Is that the real problem?' I enquire.

'Er … yes.'

'Are you sure?'

'Yes.'

So we clear the decks again. We know what we must do to achieve twenty on the bottom line, and we've isolated the difficulty. Now is the time to see whether the problem is insuperable. The questions virtually ask themselves. Who do we know who has faced this kind of situation in the past? What did he find? How can we handle it so the existing salesforce stays loyal? What other opportunities and bonuses can we offer them? Will they really object if we expand the salesforce, or is that simply somebody's opinion? What is the psychology of the people concerned? Is there any way we can win over the doubters?

Under this kind of interrogation, the problem tends to vaporize. Then suddenly, the pact will spring another problem: 'Actually, there's this reason as well why we can't do it.' At that point you know you've won, because the meeting has already agreed that this one obstacle (the possible objection of the company's salesforce) was all that stood in the way. 'Objective first, obstacle last' has carried you over the hump.

In reality, I would combine both approaches in planning for the future – aspiration *and* forward projection.

In any organization there are two types of people. There are those who hang on to the minimization of chance too long who say, 'This is where we are. Where can we project ourselves out to?' And then there are those who will try to maximize chance too soon: 'I know where I'd like to be, can I see any way back?'

Each has a part to play, and I'll set both groups to work to produce a plan. At the end of the exercise I'll probably have two answers. The first group will say, 'We've taken n reference points, we've done mathematical projections, we've tossed around squares and root formulae, we've computerized the data, ground it up, everything you could think of, and we predict 10 per cent growth.' The second group might then respond, 'We're pretty hopeful; we don't know how we got here, but we've seen an opportunity and we think we could be looking at 40 per cent growth.'

I'll then bring the two teams together and analyze the gap. Those who have clung to every reality will probably find themselves being drawn upwards, while the high-flyers will start to moderate. The most effective plan is likely to be found somewhere in the middle.

5. *Know when to stop planning and start implementing.*

Judgement, as we've seen, is a series of transitions – from gathering information to assessing it; from assessment to planning; and from planning to implementation. Having looked at the first two, we need now to study the third.

The shift from planning to implementation needs the same care in its timing as the original shift from awareness into judgement. I have worked for people who have planned down to destruction, spending more time assessing and sorting the data than fighting the competition in the marketplace. I have also encountered the wing-and-prayer merchants who act first, think second, and cannot plan to save their lives. But sometimes it's not easy to know how much planning is appropriate.

During my time at Searle, we planned to build a biotechnology plant. It was a modest-sized, tastefully designed building and the processes to be carried out inside it were entirely innocuous. The planners thought of everything: we had blueprints, photographs, models, technical specifications, the lot. In architectural, mechanical and financial terms it was very well planned indeed. Had the planning stopped there, we would all have been satisfied. But somebody thought further. To an investigative journalist, a biotechnology plant is only a fraction removed from Dr Frankenstein's laboratory with all its implications of genetic mutation and terrible biological mishaps. To forestall any adverse reaction in the press, the plan went on to include a full public-relations exercise and a community briefing programme. In due course Patrick Jenkin, the UK Secretary of State for Industry, performed the opening ceremony and the Research Director drank a glass of effluent to demonstrate the total safety of the plant.

In this case the planning was almost finished too soon, and it was only that extra piece of awareness (psychological awareness, note) that showed us we should push the planning a little further. The project was fully planned only when the last stage was bolted on.

So knowing the right *level* of planning is essential. You cannot leap too early, as we almost did with our pilot plant, nor can you let the moment pass. Minimizing chance and maximizing the chance remaining often means seizing the opportunity, and you cannot have opportunism if you cling rigidly to pre-formed plans. The solar wind we postulated in chapter two called for the revision, almost overnight, of all the company's previous production goals. Even as I write, I'm becoming aware of a personal career opportunity that may mean the most drastic revision of my plans and embroil me in all the upheaval and inconvenience that a good opportunity often entails. By the time I finish this book I may be doing things in my career that I never dreamed I would. Stay tuned!

In planning, balance is all. The day you stop doing it you're in trouble, but the day your plan becomes a bible, you're equally at risk.

CHAPTER SEVEN

The Measure Of The Man

IN LOOKING at awareness and judgement, we have, at every turn, run up against homo sapiens and his peculiar ways. Which is only to be expected, given that life's circumstances are nearly always generated by people. So let's stick with people, gather up the subject of awareness and judgement, and see how, if we wish to minimize chance and maximize the chance remaining, we must get the measure of this strange, two-legged creature.

I restate the point: nothing happens in business unless people do it. No people, no business. And most managers would agree that the single most elusive resource in any enterprise is people of the right calibre and skills. This being so, the most important managerial function must be the recruitment and development of individuals. The chairman who believes he is running a company is deluding himself. He runs it through people, and the best way he can minimize chance is to surround himself with the right people. But how many managers live by that maxim? In many companies, more time and effort goes into the car policy than into intelligent recruiting.

To recruit, you have to be aware and you have to make judgements. That much is obvious. But for years some companies have muddled along with an amateurish approach to both. They're quite good at drawing up a job specification, because that's something they know about. They're not bad, either, at creating the corresponding man specification, because they know the kind of person they would like. But the final stage – finding the man to fit the man specification – is often so casually treated as to be virtually left to chance.

People are interviewed, even for top jobs, on the back of an envelope. Soundings will be taken; there'll be lunch and a chat; but through it all, it's the behavioural rather than any objective analysis that carries the day. If I look right, the assumption is that I am right. So my first duty as a candidate is not to offend the code. I will take care not to turn up with dirty boots, snotty handkerchief and uncleaned teeth. I will try not to pick my nose or to say, 'Sorry, don't know anything about extruded tubes. Next question.' A decent suit and good personal presentation can override a host of disqualifications.

But I'm being unfair. Most recruitment interviews do look more deeply – at qualifications, career details, record in the business, and so on. But even if it's true, all such information is historical: it tells you what a person has achieved in the past, not what he's capable of doing in the future. After this kind of scrutiny, I can still walk into your company as an unknown entity and you will not know I'm incompetent until I turn up and demonstrate it. At which point you can either sack me, at enormous expense and inconvenience, or (here's the pact again) pretend that nothing is wrong and support me in my failure so as not to have to admit that you made a mistake.

I've heard it again and again: 'Poor Arnold, did frightfully well in the '70s … shame he's losing his touch.' That's code for, 'Damn it, we mucked up the selection – put him in above his level of competence.'

Once in, it is still remarkably easy for a man to rise through the organization by virtue of his contacts or by clocking up the years so that sooner or later his turn will come. Under this philosophy, there is little or no incentive for a manager to demonstrate awareness, judgement, courage or flexibility. His duty, more often, is to pick up the baton left by old Rutherford and pass it eventually to young Stibbs with as little disturbance as possible to the status quo.

I do not exaggerate. British industry is stuffed with yesterday's heroes, kept in place by the pact. And one reason is the stigma the British attach to redundancy.

American companies, interestingly, are not so afflicted. For them, redundancy is a threat, a challenge, a disruption, but it is not a stigma. Consequently American managers find it much easier to say, 'Sorry Joe, computers and finance are not your métier, go and find it somewhere else.' No-one is saying, 'You're not fit to inhabit the earth, kindly do the decent thing.' They're stating a fact – no value judgement implied. But in Britain, redundancy is so riddled with connotations of failure that managers will do anything rather than push somebody out. This is an abdication of management, and one that creates endless problems: people on the books who should not be there; costs that should not be incurred; discontent from those below whose own career paths are blocked.

Take the above-mentioned Arnold, who did so well back in the '70s until the pact promoted him beyond his capabilities. It's quite likely he was hired after a good lunch and the revelation that he played bridge – so must therefore be an intellectual sort of fellow. Nobody systematically measured his capability or his potential. He arrived, did well for a while, then failed. Now everybody knows he has failed – his bosses, his colleagues, Arnold himself. The best solution, not just for the company but also for Arnold, would be a clean break; to give him a slug of money and send him to seek his fortune somewhere else.

But what happens? The Director of Personnel calls him in and says, 'Arnold, we've got this exciting new job – Head of Administration for Rubber Bands. Will you take it?' Of course Arnold says yes. He has no option. He keeps his office, his salary, his car, because his status and length of service require it, but psychologically he's wrecked. Gazing out of his window with nothing but rubber bands for company, he turns acidic. And the poison spreads. Capable people who do not have offices or cars resent the fact that he is still there. Over time, Arnold dies the death of a thousand cuts, mesmerized by the pact and unable to wriggle free.

To break the 'yesterday's hero' syndrome, you need a means of measuring people's capability – not just backwards in time, but also forwards. And such a means exists in psychometric testing.

Psychometric testing has had a bad press. For one thing, there's a lot of the spurious article about. For another, it tends to offend the pact. 'Gobbledygook,' they'll say, 'It isn't proven. It isn't our style. How can some shrink in a white coat know more about our own people than we do ourselves?'

At a management meeting some years ago I faced just such a barrage. I replied by pulling out the minutes of five years previously.

'Gentlemen,' I said. 'I've been looking through the files. Five years ago you identified four top fliers in the organization – men who were whizz-bang-magic, worth backing to the hilt. Without exception they've now been shelved as disappointing. On the other hand, some of the people who are now doing really well were written off as having peaked. I offer you a choice. Either we test psychometrically, or we go back to recruiting on the back of an envelope.'

I'm glad to say the envelope faction lost the day.

My own introduction to psychometrics was during my last few months at Beecham. I was contemplating a move, and in the course of surveying my options went and saw a Swedish firm called Pharmacia. I didn't in the end join them, but they sent me to see an outfit called Mercuri Urval. Nobody explained why, or what would happen. They simply told me to turn up.

So I did, driving over from Wycombe to Rickmansworth and arriving at a small, modern office which I took to be one of Pharmacia's trading companies. I was shown upstairs, where a young lady sat me down at a desk, gave me a sheaf of papers and a fistful of sharpened pencils, started a stopwatch and told me I had two hours.

Evidently this was not a trading company. In front of me were sheets of 11-plus-type questions – 'Which is the odd one out?' and so on. A morning of tests was followed by an afternoon of one-to-one interviews. I quickly twigged what was going on and went through the motions with increasing scepticism. But at the end of the day I was staggered by how much they could tell me about myself. This was no mumbo-jumbo; these serious, scientific men were nothing like those fakirs who leap out at you in oriental bazaars and claim they can tell you your mother's name. I'm too long in the tooth to fall for the open-ended question where you provide the answer and they play it back later, differently worded. Amazingly, they had got through to the kind of person I really was.

I have since got to know the technique a lot better. Mercuri Urval and others like them are not psychoanalysts. They will not say, 'This man had a difficult birth experience and suffered from an overbearing father.' Their task is to measure person A against job B. They will start, therefore, with as detailed a job spec as the company concerned can provide. What will be this man's key responsibilities? What size of team will he work with? With whom is he interacting? In response they will then say, 'Joe Smith will have these difficulties but these strengths … His willingness to dominate shows he'll do this standing on his head … His low score on flexibility suggests he'll need a lot of help on that … If you don't develop him here, you'll lose him … If you don't control him there, he may create a danger …'

I find people often get nervous when I start talking psychometrics. I can see what's going through their minds. 'Damn it, he'll see I've bent a paperclip and he won't like the way I'm crossing my legs.' More seriously, the man will be thinking, 'If he sends me to Mercuri Urval, he'll discover I'm weak in finance.' Not so. Psychometrics does not measure skills so much as personal attitudes and qualities. The conclusion will not be, 'This man is a good or bad accountant,' but this man rates thus on numeracy, analytical ability, interest in solving problems, planning ability and so on. In any case, the result of uncovering such a weakness is not to slap the man's wrists; it's to make a note not to push him too much in that direction. The same process will also have revealed his strengths. Pushed in another direction, the man may have potential for travelling further than he ever thought possible.

'But is it true?' is the obvious question. I think my own doubts on that score were settled when a candidate at Mercuri Urval went hopelessly awry under sections of the test dealing with endurance and emotional stability. The people running the test actually stopped it half way through and asked him what the trouble was. It turned out he had just had a bereavement, but instead of putting off the test he had decided to go through with it. His early results flagged up the message, 'There's something strange going on here; this man's responses show he's all over the place; don't go any further.'

I'm convinced that psychometrics is a valid science, and I hold no brief for Mercuri Urval. I can simply state that in my experience it has proved a beneficial management tool. In every company I have worked in since that first encounter, I have used it as an aid to recruitment.

Of course it's not the only consideration. I still have the company's appraisals, it's reports, the records, and psychometrics perhaps contributes 20 per cent of the total picture. But that 20 per cent at least allows me to minimize chance. It offers me new awarenesses. Can this man go further? Can he change shape or direction? How will he interact – upwards, downwards, sideways? In short, it gives me another view which is not past historic. It's a prognosis – an assessment of where the man's basic fibres are likely to take him in the future.

The benefit is twofold. One, I can fit the man to the job with an extra degree of precision. Two, I know how to develop him. Having minimized luck to begin with, I am better equipped to maximize what luck has sent me anyway.

Ninty per cent of industrial training is about getting rid of weaknesses. 'Dennis is a good chap,' someone will say. 'Bit rusty on the paperwork, though. Let's send him on a course and get him put right.' So Dennis, like a car with a dodgy carburettor, is sent in to be mended. As long as recruitment is left to chance, this corrective activity will be necessary. But suppose, instead, that people are employed for their strengths and that those strengths closely match the requirements of the job. It is likely, then, that any weaknesses will have only minimal effect on performance, in which case there is no call to train them out. Resources can now be devoted to building up strengths. 'This man is whizz-bang: let's now make him magic whizz-bang.' You're no longer mending dodgy carburettors; you're tuning engines and attaching the go-faster stripes.

In short, why take misfits and iron out the distortions, when, with the help of psychometrics, you can get it right in one?

An important part of getting it right is to find the answer to these four questions:

1. *Can this man stretch to fit the job?*

Virtually every individual has to make an adjustment in order to do his or her job. The problems arise when the gap between the task and the core person becomes too great a bridge. In extreme cases you're asking Rambo to become a social worker, or St Francis of Assisi to run an abattoir. Neither of them could do it: the compensatory mechanism just would not stretch, and they'd probably make themselves ill in the attempt.

Closer to home is the classic promotional error of taking a good rep and making him a manager. The fact that is often overlooked is that being a manager requires very different skills to being a rep. Nearly always, you're asking the individual to increase his compensatory distance. Now there's nothing wrong with that as long as he has the internal resources to cope. The mistake is to put a man in that position

without first measuring the degree of stretch within him. Consequently many good reps go on to make very bad managers.

Relying solely on historical data in making appointments locks you into Peter's Principle, whereby you advance a man to his own level of incompetence (shades of Arnold and his rubber bands). You can't help it, because you don't know that a man is incompetent until he reaches a position where it shows. So you keep pushing, and inevitably you push one step too far, because that's the only way you can find out when to stop. But by then he's failed. It's like nudging people forward in the dark and noting that some drop over the edge and some do not. From where you stand you cannot tell who will succeed and who will disappear from view.

The past offers very little guidance as to future performance. Not every rep who's made a manager fails, and some failed reps even make good managers. What's missing under Peter's Principle is the realization that you're often asking people to do a completely *different* job to the one they were doing before. The question then is, what do you know about the man that will indicate his suitability for this job as well as that one? In other words, what is his ability to compensate?

When a person compensates, he's drawing on inner reservoirs of energy and endurance. The more of these he uses up, the less he has available for other, more productive activities. The right man in the right job will therefore have more energy for the task than the misfit: he'll probably also be more stable, mentally and emotionally. By measuring a person's stability and endurance, his willingness to dominate, his attitude to new responsibility and so on, psychometrics can give a useful pointer as to whether man A in job B will in fact be able to deliver.

2. *Is this man more interested in people or tasks?*

Psychometrics can also reveal whether a given individual is task-orientated or person-orientated. A successful business needs people of both types, so it behoves the manager to know which sort of person he is dealing with.

In reality, most people are a mixture of both. We all have tasks to perform, whether it's tying a shoelace at the age of four or running a company at forty-four. In carrying out any task, it helps to recognize the rights and feelings of other people, otherwise there is no society. So most of the time we go about our tasks with a degree of circumspection and sensitivity.

There are some who don't, of course. I suspect that Attila the Hun was not all that person-orientated: he certainly got his tasks done efficiently. His modern counterpart is possibly the Air Force major, deputed to build an aerodrome on some Phillipino island. You'll have seen him in the movies if not in reality – clenched cigar; John Wayne face; a battery of bulldozers behind him grinding up the huts of the villagers. Three days later, it's tarmac from shore to shore and B52s flying in and out of the aerodrome. Never mind the human devastation; the end justifies the means.

The contrary, person-orientated attitude is expressed by the employee who says, 'I'm afraid I haven't got the budget done, Mr Burke, but the accountant's wife has just had a baby and I didn't want to call him out over the Christmas break.'

For my part, I try to strike an even balance between people and task at the start of a project. Later, as deadlines approach, I begin to come down on the task. I would not, I think, kill to get a budget out on time (jobs have to be done through people, after all), but I nevertheless start to turn the screw on quality, performance and schedule. Others, I've noticed, will dismantle targets and strategies if they start to get awkward for the people concerned.

Here, as with other areas of your psychology, knowing which way you tend is bound to make you a better manager. At the very least, it will tell you when your own predilection is showing and allow you to compensate if need be. It will also help you to swing the emphasis from one end of the spectrum to the other as the task in hand requires.

More useful still is to extend this type of awareness to others. We've looked at Arnold, yesterday's hero, pushed into limbo to look after rubber bands. Let's now concentrate on Ted, who happens to be Arnold's boss.

Ted has been heard to bemoan his luck: 'It's terribly unfortunate, but we've got all these managers who've been here thirty years and we can't dislodge them.' I would first say to Ted that he cannot blame chance. The situation exists because over the years he and his department have built up a paternalistic, person-orientated culture without realizing they were doing so. The crime is not in the culture: a paternalistic, person-orientated culture may be entirely appropriate. The crime, rather, is not to be aware that the departmental culture is of this type. Until that awareness exists, the problem cannot be identified, let alone solved.

So how can Ted be made aware? And what difference would it make?

If I were Ted's boss, I would challenge him. 'How come,' I'd say, 'you're still employing Arnold?'

The answer would no doubt be a sad shake of the head. 'He's a problem, I know. But Arnold's been here all this time. He's a nice guy, and he hasn't done anything wrong. He's just not very good at his job. I've given him Rubber Bands. What else can I do?'

I now have a choice.

I can point out to Ted that whether or not he knows it, he's a person-orientated manager and he needs to redress the balance. 'Get in there,' I might say, 'and tell Arnold he's fired.' This option makes logical sense but it does have problems. Ted is fifty-six. He's been person-orientated all his life and he isn't going to change now. If I tell him straight out to fire Arnold, all he can draw on is naked courage to help him to do it.

My other option is to work on Ted's strengths, not his limitations. 'Fine,' I could say. 'You've given Arnold everything he's ever needed. In fact you've looked after him extremely well – you're that sort of person. But do you realize that you've ruined thirty other people who haven't been able to advance because Arnold is blocking the way?'

This is not an entirely hypothetical case. I have been in this position, and the effect of that simple observation has been startling. Immediately, the man's paternalism is in top gear. Aware of what he has done, he can now ride into action on his own natural qualities. His concern for people has been activated, and his call on courage – a facility he probably doesn't have in any great measure – is that much less.

Take a caveman from the jungle and fly him up in a helicopter: he'll be terrified. With no awareness of what a helicopter is, and therefore no means of judging if he'll come down alive, courage is all he has. The pilot, on the other hand, knows all about helicopters and has made the judgement that he will land safely. The courage he requires is relatively little. Moral: make your own people aware of their psychological leaning; fix it so they're motivated by what comes naturally to them; and you'll increase their courage and their flexibility.

3. Can this man interact with those around him?

Besides measuring the compensatory ability and the task/person bias of each individual, psychometrics can help you place your people so that they integrate. The trick is not simply to ensure that the man is right for the job. It is also to match up the layers – to get manager A reporting to a particular kind of boss while managing particular kinds of people himself.

To take it one stage further, you can spread the integration sideways so that members of a board, for example, form a good fit alongside each other. I'm not talking here about installing yes-men or sacrificing proper judgement for an easy life. Quite the contrary.

Imagine your company or department as a system of connecting pipes, each section of pipe an individual. Through this system, information (i.e. awareness) flows upwards, downwards and sideways. It's important that each section of pipe is in the right place and of the right specification – in other words, that the people match the jobs they have to do. It's also important that the joins between the pipes are in good working order, otherwise valuable information will be blocked or sprayed uselessly all over the premises.

I knew of a serious case of 'blockage' when a senior finance man decided to close his discipline to outsiders and virtually ceased communicating with the rest of the world. The finance directorate became a closed shop, a black hole, a thing whose function was not known and which was therefore viewed with intense suspicion by other people in the company. Before long it was failing to service the other disciplines as it should and instead became a policeman of the worst kind. Naturally, other departments became less disposed to co-operate, so data going into the finance directorate dwindled to a trickle. Information coming out was therefore inaccurate. The department became all mechanics and no creativity. Instead of being seen as a useful ally by the rest of the company, it became an internal enemy that everybody tried to avoid.

When I talk about 'integration' to ease the flow of awareness, I mean an ideal juxtaposition of psychologies – one that allows the information to pass with minimum distortion, that increases the corporate level of awareness and so makes right judgement more likely. Psychometrics is the best tool I have yet found for achieving this end.

4. Can this man bring a fresh mind to the problems?

Psychometrics, finally, can widen your scope when you're trawling for candidates.

It's a common misconception that the best person for a given job has to come from within the industry. I suspect we think that way because we overvalue awareness. 'What do you know about extruded tube technology, Mr Smith? Absolutely everything? Welcome on board.' Indeed, the back-of-the-envelope school has nothing else to go on, for judgement, courage and flexibility are vaguer concepts and far more difficult to measure.

People take diplomas in tube technology and can hold up pieces of paper to demonstrate their awareness. There are no diplomas in judgement. Yet judgement, courage and flexibility are just as important as management qualities. To go by awareness only is to back one against three. Result: constipation, dullness, the repeat of history. But find someone outside the industry who has judgement, courage and flexibility, and all he will lack is one of the four. What's more, awareness is the one that matters least, because it's the easiest to acquire. That's what libraries are for, and the gathering of knowledge becomes easier all the time with the explosion in information technology.

In any case, the raw material of industry is people: the man who knows about people in retail will know about people in plastics.

'All right, clever clogs,' says the pact. 'Fetch someone from aerospace and stick him in pharmaceuticals. All that will happen is that meeting will be twice as long because he doesn't know the industry vocabulary. He'll say, "Why don't you do this?" and we'll have to explain that it isn't possible for reasons A, B, C and D.'

To which I reply, 'That's precisely the fellow's gift. He's fresh, so he can't build in the obstacles at the beginning.'

G.D. Searle used to make – in fact still make – a laxative called Metamucil. It's made from isphagula, a cotton-like plant that grows in India. You treat it, you blow ethylene oxide through it, and you end up with a powdery substance in a carton. When you're taking it, you pour in water and give it a stir and you end up with a jug of wallpaper paste. You need to be a hero to drink it, because it has to go down in one go. It's effective, though. Down in the lower bowel it bulks out and usually solves the problem.

Metamucil has been Searle's biggest product in the USA for years, and we in the UK were constantly being pressed to get it moving in our own market. We had tried, but again and again the product had flopped.

Then a fresh mind came in – a senior manager who had barely encountered the product in his life (lucky man!) and so lacked any prior awareness of the subject. At once he saw the answer, and like all the best answers it was simple. He mixed the basic goo with some effervescent material to make it sparkly, added a bit of lime juice for taste, and packed it in fancy new aluminium sachets with an attractive design on the front. Suddenly it looked good, was pleasant to take, and started selling. The outside eye, unclouded by prejudice, had fixed on the real obstacles and seen what to do.

Managing 6,000 people as I do, a large proportion of whom are graduates and second-degree students, I simply could not survive if I relied on knowledge alone. My own academic achievements would barely qualify me to sweep the boardroom, but that fact matters not one jot. I and my staff borrow from each other. With my judgement I can take the other person's data and say, 'That doesn't hold,' or 'Why don't you try that?' He then takes my judgement and applies it to his discipline. It is also my task to feed in courage and flexibility. Should we ever discover that a fertile solar wind had bathed the earth, I would be responsible for gearing up production of baby products by the incredible thousandfold.

My ignorance is my strength, because it stops me putting up obstacles at the beginning. Instead, I can say to the experts, 'You guard me against errors of fact. I will bring an unjaundiced eye to the problem and contribute judgemental skills, courage and flexibility.'

What's more, I try to employ managers with the same gifts. With psychometrics, I have a means at my disposal for measuring judgement, courage and flexibility, so I'm freed from relying on awareness as the only criterion for my choice. My net is therefore wider, and the team that I can build around me is likely to be better as a result.

CHAPTER EIGHT

Be Brave

A WARENESS IS relatively easy to harness. Judgement, although more difficult to acquire, can nevertheless be learnt if you put your mind to it. Together, awareness and judgement enable you to extend your control over circumstance and so reduce your vulnerability to chance.

But we would not want to obliterate luck even if we could. After all, a moment of luck, properly handled, can carry you further and faster than years of hard work. The skill is to recognize luck for what it is (using awareness and judgement), and then to make the most of it.

Now we come to new ground. As we slide from minimizing chance to maximizing the chance remaining, we enter the territory of those other two qualities, courage and flexibility. These now become your tools.

Beady-eyed awareness and unfettered judgement may have dictated the most extraordinary courses of action: multiply production a thousandfold in response to that solar wind; send a Chinese-speaking MD to Latin America; stop making widgets and start making underseal flange sprockets ... Nothing is out of the question when awareness and judgement have been properly applied. But to turn aspiration into reality needs courage and flexibility. As it happens, these are the most difficult of the four qualities to acquire.

No matter. What we must not do is throw up our hands and say, 'You've either got courage and flexibility or you haven't.' That is simply to surrender to chance. Instead, let us apply the minimization/maximization principle – see what we can do to net these qualities in, then consider how to make the most of the courage and flexibility we have.

We start with courage.

The difficult thing about courage is that it's virtually impossible to programme into your organization. Indeed, you usually cannot tell whether or not you have it until suddenly you need it – and it's either there or it isn't.

By definition, bravery comes into play once you have crossed the border between control and uncontrol. If everything is taped down and you're truly in command, your call on courage will be small. And of course the whole point of the minimization of chance is to get things taped down as much as possible and to ensure that you are in command. It follows that the good manager of luck will need less courage in his day-to-day work than his free-wheeling counterpart who leaves his success to chance.

But even though we push back the moment, the time will inevitably come when we're over the frontier and bravery is required. Your awareness and judgement tell you that you've reached a confluence of events. You've done what you can to control the outcome (it's probably not *all* you could have done, but it's all you could do in the time) and the things left undone must stay undone. It's all or nothing. You're out of fuel, you're on the glide path, and you'll either make it or you won't. The bravery applies to the only decision you have left – whether to bale out and cut your losses, or stay strapped in and see whether fate will bring you safely to the ground.

If you can force your heart and nerve and sinew
To serve your turn long after they are gone,
And so hold on when there is nothing in you
Except the Will which says to them, 'Hold on!'

... you know you're being brave.

But before we think about exercising bravery, let's move the definition closer in so we know what kind of beast we're handling.

To begin with, we're not talking about recklessness. The good businessman, like the good chess player, is not playing the next move, he's sixteen moves ahead. And he knows that if he doesn't make a certain move against a certain standard of play, he'll never recover. In chess tournaments you sometimes see a player retire quite early in the game. It isn't faint-heartedness; it's the knowledge that he's made a wrong move, and, because he can see ahead, he knows the mistake is irreversible. So he might as well pull out and save everybody an hour's hard work.

Bravery in business is not Charge-of-the-Light-Brigade valour: I don't believe in plunging towards the guns if the only possible outcome is a cannonball between the eyes. Courage must be tempered with judgement and it has to hold out at least the possibility of success before it is worth indulging. As we noted earlier, the best *living* racing drivers have bravery and judgement in fine balance: too much of either makes it hardly worth continuing.

I once knew a middle manager whose bosses (there were two of them) insisted on giving him unreasonable targets that could only be met if he himself bullied those below him. As one of the juniors in question, I was only too aware of the pressure he was under. He resisted his bosses at every opportunity, but did so with an acute lack of awareness or judgement. Even I had a better understanding of his bosses' psychology than he did. Flexibility was denied him because his adversaries would not be budged, so all he had left was courage. The result was, he continued fighting cases beyond their usefulness and got dismissed. He was too brave to be helpful. He not only lost the battle but lost the war, for those he was trying to protect, myself among them, were now left with no protection at all.

So courage in business is not the same as recklessness. Nor does it always mean *doing* something. Nothing spurs you into action so much as a setback. Your plans have gone awry; you're in a corner; and the only solution, apparently, is to rush out with guns blazing. Perhaps we're conditioned by our physiology. If someone sticks a pin in your hand, you'll move it; if you're threatened where you are, you'll get yourself somewhere else as quickly as you can. People *feel* brave when their backs are against the wall and find themselves doing things they never thought they could. But to leap straight into action when faced with a threat is not necessarily the bravest thing to do.

I have seen the impulse at work with colleagues who favour the instant action reaction. A problem occurs and the question is immediately, 'What are you going to do, John?' It's assumed I'll do something, because to be seen doing nothing is unacceptable. If I then say, 'Nothing,' my colleagues are aghast.

'But can't you see there's a crisis?' (As they'd say in the movies, 'Don't you know there's a war on?')

'Of course,' say I. 'I just don't think this is the time to evoke those forces.'

'Why not?'

'Well, the situation may go this way, it may go that way. We'll know in a few days. I want to keep my freedom to act next week. If I act now, I'll deny myself that freedom.'

You can see them twitching as they come to terms with the logic. A case in point was when I was working for Searle in the United States and the British authorities were about to ban one of our products. Instant action: the move had to be blocked. A project team was assembled, airline tickets were booked, and calls were made to London saying, 'Tell the Minister we're on the way.'

I knew, for my part, that this full-frontal approach would simply irritate the Minister in question and be counter-productive. In any case, the British Government had other decisions to make before it went ahead with the ban, and I knew that the results might provide a precedent we could use. So I advised sending the project team home.

In the event, the tactic worked.

My colleagues, however, were extremely uncomfortable: 'What does this guy think he's doing?' The fact is, awareness and judgement in this instance dictated inaction, not action – a course that was far more taxing on the nerves and actually required more bravery than the alternative.

So courage may mean doing nothing.

Just as contrary to our basic instincts is to act when things are going well. 'Don't tamper with a well-running machine,' said Colin Chapman of Lotus Cars. I take his point. If things are going well, you may only worsen them if you interfere. But we're talking here about maximizing what chance has brought along. If events have turned out in your favour, the key to enlarging your luck may well be to do something further.

Take our MD of Babybounce in the aftermath of that solar wind. To maximize his luck, he must boost production to meet the expected demand. But while he's about it, he can also introduce a new *type* of plant, able to produce the quality and range of merchandise that his marketing people have been wanting for years but which previous volumes could never justify. It's that old alchemy of luck turning into more luck as you get to work on it.

Of course you will need to analyze. I'm all for judging the situation and deciding to do nothing; the unforgivable thing is to make your decision without analysis. Solar winds aside, it's unlikely that the circumstances you're enjoying are wholly down to luck. They'll result from things you have done or not done, or from things other people have done or not done. If you can identify what those things are, you may be able to increase your luck, or repeat it, or turn it on to order. Without such analysis, you're reduced to waiting for that conjunction of circumstances to come round again. It's a choice between astronomy and astrology; control and passivity.

But acting to enlarge good luck can require just as much courage as not acting in the face of bad luck. If your engine happens to be winning races, and you've worked out *why* it's winning races, and you know what to do to make it win more races, you'd damn well better be right. No-one is ordering you to take the engine apart and rebuild it, and no-one would mind particularly if you didn't. You volunteer the action at your peril and it's on your head if you fail.

But without exercising courage in this way, you cannot make the most of what chance has given you. Your luck will wash in and wash out, and you'll have missed an opportunity to increase it.

So courage is not recklessness. It's summoning the will to act or not act, whichever is appropriate, in the light of awareness and judgement.

Furthermore, nearly all business courage is psychological, not physical. It may sound obvious, but it's worth stating. In my years as a manager, I have not yet had to walk a tightrope across Niagara or swim through shark-infested seas. I have, however, had to face up to people. Whether this is harder or easier than demonstrating physical courage I don't know. I suspect there's no difference. But over the years I've identified two psychological ogres that will have you for breakfast if you don't stand up and face them (and sometimes if you *do* stand up and face them).

The first is that old enemy, the pact. To appreciate its power, try this exercise if you don't mind losing your job.

You're in a meeting; the pressure is on; the clock is whizzing round. As the screws come down, watch the smokers. They'll start patting their shirts and their trouser pockets, perhaps not even aware that they're doing so. Two or three minutes later, the first cigarettes will appear. Now is your moment. Open your drawer and pull out a bottle of Scotch. Pour yourself two fingers into a glass, screw back the top and put the bottle away. You'll have the undivided attention of everyone in the room. Which is absurd. All you're doing is substituting one drug for another, but such is the weight of opinion that smokes are acceptable in meetings and drinks are not, that this simple action seems perverse in the extreme.

Whichever front you're working on – awareness, judgement, courage, flexibility – the pact will come back at you and say, 'Sorry old boy, it's not our style ... just not the way we do things round here.' There may come a time when your only weapon against the pact is naked courage.

The second ogre is called Whim, and he tends to inhabit the upper echelons of management.

The higher you go in the corporate structure, the more you come across individuals with enormous personal power. I have known bosses whose revenue levels, whose freedom to travel the world, whose powers to make and break were awesome. For whatever reason – it may be boredom as much as anything – awareness sometimes slips at those levels and self-delusion creeps in. Decisions start to be governed as much by whim as by awareness and judgement. And it's not a trait confined to businessmen. Witness those TV anchor-men whose sign-offs get increasingly eccentric, not to mention the politicians who start to believe their own propaganda.

Perhaps we should expect this kind of behaviour. However big these men are, however much braid they have on their collars, they are only human and they have their frailties and quirks. Arguably, the line between greatness and madness is a fine one. Be that as it may, the good manager must recognize whim when he sees it and know how to respond.

As always, the first requirement is awareness. Whim comes in many guises: rarely does the big man flash you a slide labelled, *My whim today – for your information*. The whim element must be disentangled from the man's whole thesis.

You must then decide whether to bow to that whim or resist it. The criterion, in my view, is how much it costs. Take the corporation president who enjoys making the throwaway remark of self-depreciation: 'Don't mind me, guys, I'm only the president.' It's an act, and it requires someone to say, 'Come now, sir.' One time in five I'll give him the pat he needs, because it costs nothing, changes nothing, and doesn't stop me being my own man. But if a president were to say, 'I want you to fix a job for my brother-in-law in your marketing department', I would have to refuse. It would change things, gobble me up, as it were, stop me from being in charge of myself. In those circumstances it's courage that must carry the day.

The imponderable in all of this is whether you can add to the amount of courage in people's make-up, or whether the most you can do is draw out the courage that's already there.

We all know that in times of crisis people exceed their apparent bravery quota. That's not because they're unafraid; on the contrary, you cannot be brave unless you are afraid. The neighbour who dashes into a burning house to rescue a child, or the soldier storming a machine-gun nest, gets his bravery in one of two ways. Either he has more courage than he thought (people misjudge their levels of everything, including courage), or he's driven by a moral code probably instilled in childhood. When there's no time to think, you'll go into action on auto-pilot and do things you wouldn't have done if you'd had the chance to reflect.

In business, for better or worse, you rarely need these spontaneous dollops of bravery. That's probably a consequence of business courage being psychological rather than physical. Usually there's ample time for thought in the run-up to being brave. You sit in the oaken boardroom staring at the lines of grey-haired men; everyone is polite (usually); your bravery, when it comes, must be on your initiative for no-one will catapult you into it.

It's the bravery of the bomber pilot over the fighter pilot. The fighter pilot scrambles on the bell, is airborne in thirty seconds and knows he'll be down in half an hour – alive or otherwise. In the meantime he's too busy lining up his gun-sights to be scared. But the bomber pilot has ten hours in the freezing cold alone with his thoughts before anything happens to distract him, so has all the time in the world to become as frightened as he likes. What counts is his mental and emotional stability. Can he, despite being frightened, get his aircraft to the target at precisely 03.20 hours?

I think it probable that the level of bravery we were born with cannot be greatly altered. The skill of management is therefore to draw out and harness the courage that already exists in people. If you can do so, the rewards can be far-reaching.

Let me quote yet another case where a pharmaceutical

product was threatened with banning. (It doesn't happen every day, I assure you!) The authority's reasoning was perfectly valid for the family of products it sought to ban, but not in our case. It was only the imprecise wording of the clause that extended the ban to our own, perfectly innocuous product. We decided that the medical department should contest the ban. This would mean going before the grey eminences of the medical profession – a knee-knocking experience, and one that would need a great deal of courage. The individuals concerned went in, stood their ground, made a strong case and lost. No matter. Honour was salvaged, and the team, having been brave once, was well prepared for future occasions when bravery would be needed again.

Raising the corporate level of bravery is a matter of awareness and judgement. Bravery is a corporate resource. Even if you cannot create it, you must know how much you have and how it is distributed.

Be aware of what you are letting in through your doors. If you didn't want Attila the Hun in your organization, what the hell is he doing there? Be absolutely sure you do want him before you hire him, because by definition he's going to sweep away any obstacle (and that could mean you) to get to his goal. And once he's in, allow him to be brave. Many companies employ brave people, then straightjacket them through fear of the consequences.

One of the best product managers I ever knew was an intelligent, creative, brave individual as the best product managers are. But in working for a pharmaceutical company he was in an industry that must always be careful. As it happened, he was burdened with a management that was cautious even for the industry. While his agile brain invented opportunities for the company, his room for manoeuvre became narrower and narrower as management restricted his freedom. In the end, not prepared to be neutered, he resigned. The company, though it needed him badly, breathed a sigh of relief.

To have brave people throttled by timid management is absurd. (To the aware, that sigh of relief was more like a death rattle.) It usually ends in upheaval: the fellow takes his courage elsewhere, leaving the corporate stock depleted and the bosses complaining bitterly of 'the viper in our bosom'.

Psychometric testing, as I've suggested, gives you about 20 per cent of the overall picture in recruitment and development. It tells you almost nothing of a man's awareness (you can find that out by other means); it starts to fill in the picture on judgement and flexibility, and provides virtually all your information by the time you get to the courage box. So use it. How ready is this person to accept responsibility? How dominant is he? Is he interested in solving problems? Is he a go-getter who likes to do things on his own initiative, or is he happier responding to instructions? How well compensated is he? Does he have reservoirs of endurance and stability? All these are pointers to a person's level of courage, and all can be measured.

Having gone through the awareness stage and deployed your people accordingly, the next step is to strip away the hindrances to courage. You may not be able to make people braver, but you can at least release whatever courage they have.

You can start by removing the penalties, so that even the least brave can have a go without fear of reprisals if they get it wrong. By now, one hopes, you will have about you people who are capable of judgement, so lifting the penalties ought not to signal chaos. Having chosen them for their judgement, trust them to tread wisely. Furthermore, if your people are aware, they'll be able to see your objectives, so they should be braver in facing up to change. Add to these ingredients a free-speaking culture that encourages people to say what they think, and your corporate bravery gauge ought to run pretty high.

Good leadership beings out people's courage. A sign of successful management is when your own staff surprise themselves with what they find they can do.

All that said, no-one can expect others to be brave unless he himself sets the example. Awareness and judgement will help you to be brave – or, at least, will shift the boundary between the territory you know and control (territory you can inhabit without particularly needing to be brave) and the territory you do not control and which calls for bravery as you enter it.

I have one last tip for those crossing the border: that is, live through the thing you fear. Say to yourself, 'What is it I'm afraid of? I'm afraid that this man, with this clout, will exhibit this whim ... I know it's a possibility because I've studied his psychology, and the consequences might be A, B or C.'

Get on your own somewhere, loosen the tie, engage the imagination and live through the worst possible scenario. Nothing is ever as frightening as the unknown. Playing the film in your mind at least reduces that element. Ask yourself, 'Which way do I really think it will go? Is there any way, even at this stage, that I can influence the outcome? Can I handle the worst? In the end, is this a risk to avoid or take?' Let all the questions pass through your head. Then do what your judgement tells you.

I find it works. One of the worst periods of my working life was the transition from Beecham to Searle; from a British company where I understood the codes and culture to an American organization whose rules I initially didn't understand. My predicament was not helped by political manoeuvrings going on over my head. I knew they were significant but I couldn't comprehend them, and for a few weeks I felt completely at sea.

At the time I don't think anybody noticed the struggle I was facing to keep ahead of the job. That's because every lunch time I would go home, face my fears, run through the worst possible outcome in my mind and try to enter the psychology of those who were making life so difficult. Through this kind of discipline, I found it possible to recover my nerve in time to address the next set of obstacles.

However thorough your preparation, you may still be scared. In fact, you probably will be. But you can at least be confident of the process that has brought you to this point. It may be unknown territory on the other side, but the decision to cross is yours and you have your reasons for it.

CHAPTER NINE

The Flex Factor

THROUGH AWARENESS and judgement you have pushed back the frontiers of your own control. You have also taken steps to raise the level of corporate bravery, so that failure of nerve does not prevent you exploiting the opportunities that are offered. You can look at circumstance as it confronts you, judge how to act, and know that your people will follow you down whatever route you choose.

There is one missing ingredient: flexibility. Awareness, judgement and courage will get you nowhere if, when the decision is made, your people and systems are not sufficiently flexible to put it into action.

In seeking flexibility, we are not looking for people who will bend to every wind. An eighteenth-century wit likened George II to a cushion, bearing the imprint of the last person to have sat on him. George II, it need hardly be said, was not a brilliant manager. Nor was the politician who reputedly told his audience, 'Those are my principles, but if you don't like them I can change them.' Flexibility is not the same as spinelessness. What we are seeking to achieve – in ourselves and in others – is flexibility of direction; a capacity to follow the course that awareness and judgement have set. This is often not easy. All change is loss, as they say at the Levinson

Institute. If you're going to be flexible, you're going to change things, and people, by and large, do not like change.

They will argue otherwise. 'Of course I like change,' says the Lancashire millworker. 'I go to Spain each summer for my holidays.' But the point is, he goes every year, probably to the same place, and always comes back. Nothing is very different as a result. The change that follows in the train of flexibility is more often a permanent shift. It's not about two-week holidays, but about uprooting your family and moving from Lancashire to Devon.

In my experience, Americans are more flexible in this regard than the British. A man will transfer from New England to Texas more routinely than his British counterpart from one county to the next – or even to another place of work six miles away. So the unions on the one hand, the pact on the other, dig in their heels and protest that the country's problems must be solved with everyone in place. The inflexibility is not only geographic, it's mental. While the British argued whether setting a conduit in a ship's hull to carry electric wiring was an electrician's job or a welder's, Korea took over the shipbuilding industry.

'All change is loss': the loss in question is the dissolution of familiar surroundings; of the firm base on which you once stood. For the manager, such a loss not only makes the present uncomfortable but the future less predictable. In losing his landmarks he has lost his ability to prognosticate.

All my own career moves have involved loss of one sort or another. As I've indicated, the transfer from Beecham to Searle was particularly difficult. Beecham had been my base for twelve years, and I'd grown used to its cool, well-oiled, unhurried style. The disadvantage of those qualities was that Beecham found it difficult to exploit opportunities. Searle was the opposite – less structured, fast on its feet, far more interested in the bottom line, opportunistic and aggressive, all of which you'd expect with Anatole Schwieger at the helm. The shock was considerable.

The Levinson maxim continues, 'All loss must be mourned.' In other words, the sensible response to change is

not to duck it or resent it, but to recognize that certain psychological consequences will follow and to give these room in your forward planning.

At Searle I had to recognize that, for all Beecham did well or less well, this was not Beecham. Beecham was somewhere else and it wasn't going to come back. I had to get to grips with the new situation, just as you do after a bereavement. A change of job is, in some ways, a mini-bereavement. For a while you can't adjust because habit keeps taking over and you handle situations as though the old order still existed. That's when you feel the loss, because you reach out for the known dynamic and it isn't there. You may have to reach out many times before you lose the habit, and it may take months or years before your reflex has adjusted.

When my father died, my mother was for selling the home and leaving it. I understood the impulse, but I advised her to stay where she was. The home she was in had 'husband' in it. If she moved somewhere else, she would not be able to see that he was no longer there. Taking herself away might have provided temporary comfort, but she would never have finished the mourning process. Mourning must be worked out of the system, and it takes time. There are no short cuts.

So if, as a manager, you're presiding over change, it is wise to allow people the space and time they need to get used to it. Don't hurry them. Occasionally you must actually slow them down, for some individuals will try to make an instant severance and be done with the mourning process in one go. It doesn't work. The only way through it is through it.

Recognizing the threat that flexibility can pose, yet knowing we need it, how do we set about acquiring it?

Part of the answer we have already, for flexibility distils from improved awareness and judgement. The more data you have gathered, and the better you have judged it, the more options you will see. What's more, because you have understood the reasons for change, it will seem less threatening and you won't need as much raw courage as you might otherwise have done. So potentially you're already more flexible.

But potential is one thing, practice is another. Many managers pay lip service to flexibility but fail to make the cultural and organizational changes that will encourage people to be flexible.

The first thing to do is to stop putting the obstacles at the start and to encourage others to behave similarly. If all the problems come at the beginning, flexibility will be nil: 'I can't do this because ...'

Anatole Schwieger was a master at pushing you out and getting you to do things you never thought you could. He'd paint huge canvases with nine-inch brushes in vivid colours. 'Be creative,' he'd say. 'Spend money, freak out, do this, do that.' Sometimes I couldn't believe what was happening to me as he shot me around the world and beat my parochialism out of me.

I found myself one day on a little eight-seater plane bucketing through stormy skies on a flight from Helsinki to Pori on the west coast of Finland. My mission was bizarre. I had to visit a man at Ottu Kumpu, the copper mining company, to talk about buying a few grammes of copper pulled into wire with a silver core down the middle. We needed some in one of our laboratories, and Ottu Kumpu was one of the few companies in the world with the technology to produce it. Having arrived, I sat in a small, wooden office and looked out at great cliffs of copper ingots rising into the sky like the sides of ships.

'Er, I'd like some copper,' I began.

The man gestured lazily out of the window. 'Copper? You said copper? Have you seen how much I've got?'

I admitted that I had. 'Actually,' I continued, 'I wasn't wanting all that much. How much is it per gramme?'

The man looked blank. He had no idea. His business, after all, was tonnes, not grammes. So I told him how much my copper and silver devices would earn and how much value I could add to each of those grammes.

We did a deal.

Flying back I thought, Why am I here? What's a boy from Oldham doing in Finland talking about grammes of copper with silver down the middle to a man who deals with it in shiploads? The answer, of course, was Anatole Schwieger.

His style, not surprisingly, had its challenges. For all his broad canvases, his exhortations to step out and be creative, he could simultaneously turn right the other way about, holding me down to the last cent on my balance sheet and demanding it be accounted for. Which at first was very confusing. It made it difficult to define my boundaries, and I was never quite sure where penalties might be lurking – to the detriment, I'm sure, of my flexibility.

Boundaries, then, are the next requisite for flexibility. People need to know the limits within which they can experiment without fear of penalties. There is no freedom without frontiers. Fling those frontiers as wide as you can, encourage people to range freely within them, but make sure they know where those frontiers are.

The third requisite follows from the second: there must be frank speaking, feedback, cross-fertilization and an emphasis on lateral thinking. These are all ingredients of awareness, and the more they happen the more flexible people are likely to be.

Having created an environment within which flexibility can flourish, the next step is to introduce individuals who are temperamentally capable of flexing. All the encouragement in the world will be no use at all if the human material is resistant to change. Here we're back to recruitment and psychometric testing. A person's flex-factor can be measured, arcane as it may sound. Other things being equal, to employ the flexible rather than the intransigent will make you better able to manage your luck.

In the end, however hard you try, you will never achieve total flexibility within your organization. There must come a time when you've done all you can – fed in awareness and judgement, created the right environment, found the right people – and must get down to work with the human material you have.

How do you do that?

I answer the question by re-running my thesis. Be aware,

first of all, of the kind of individuals you have about you, then exercise judgement as to how to place and manage them.

It isn't only the trade unionist who is intransigent. In many cases it is the conservative middle manager who has always done things a certain way and is not going to change now. He'd be offended if you compared him to the trade unionist, but his throttle on the company is no less destructive. He's cemented in place, and the reason is usually a point of insecurity in his own psyche. At the very least, I as a manager ought to understand what that insecurity is. I may not be able to do anything about it, but I can bear it in mind when considering how to deploy him.

On the other hand, I may have an individual whose flexibility is outweighed by his dominance. His psychometric testing has perhaps given him an assertiveness score of nine against three for flexibility. I know that once I wind him up and point him, he'll tear through the obstacles like a tornado. That may be just what the company needs. The trouble is that he'll only go in one direction. Come the day when the circumstances change and he has to take a different direction, he may end up smacking into something.

I once had an excellent salesman, and the qualities that made him so good were his singleness of mind, his tenacity, his dominance and assertiveness, and the strength of his task-orientation over his people-orientation. He sounds frightening but he wasn't, for these qualities were so well controlled and polished that his customers never felt he was overwhelming them. His limitation was that he could only keep the act up for short periods of time – which is fine when you're in and out of your customers' offices selling things, but is not much good when, as this fellow was, you're promoted to manager.

In his new job, he became a classic victim of Peter's Principle: 'Here's a good salesman; we'll make him a manager of salesmen.' Now his task was to get other people to do things and he simply couldn't shift into that mode. In due course, for all his drive and purposefulness, he was beaten down by the aggravation and annoyance that he himself generated around him. He failed – or, to be more precise, those who promoted him failed. An analysis of *why* he was such a good salesman ought to have flagged 'inflexibility' as one of the reasons – which should have raised doubts about his suitability for promotion. But no such analysis was carried out; Peter's Principle ran its course; and the man was wrongly placed.

With every instance of inflexibility, the question to ask is whether the individual can compensate. The truly inflexible man simply cannot do it. He has reached the end of his compensatory tether. His reservoirs of energy and endurance have run dry. He's brittle, and if you make him change, you'll break him. If that's the case, and he's in the way, the kindest thing to do is move him to a job where inflexibility is a virtue – the bought ledgers department, for example, where routines must be followed come what may.

Put inflexible people in inflexible jobs: it sounds obvious. But it can't be done without measuring the flex factor in the first place.

That's a complicated process, for a person's degree of flexibility is often concealed, even from himself. All of us project an image of ourselves to the outside world. If you were to meet me, you would know nothing about me other than the image I projected – and I would know nothing about you other than your image. By and large, we're all trying to be seen at our best, so there's often a gap between the image and the truth.

Like the forceshield on Starship Enterprise, the image becomes a protective coating against the buffeting of the environment. Keeping it in place requires energy – mental and ultimately physical energy. That energy, as we've seen, has to come from our own internal reservoirs. The more energy we use propping up the shield, the less we have available for the everyday business of life. So the person whose self-esteem is low, but who's busily pushing out a competent, sophisticated image, is burning a lot of energy that might better be directed to his job.

Inevitably, if you're using a lot of energy in one direction, you'll try to save it in another. And one way of saving energy is to be inflexible. If you only do two things three ways, you've released a lot of capacity. If every challenge that's brought to your desk is met with Solution A or Solution B and no other, the energy expended per working day will be low.

On the other hand, if you're intent on opening your mind every time and investigating all possibilities, you'll need a great deal of energy and you'll probably come home shattered at the end of the day. If you're compensating at the same time for a poor self-image, you're burning the candle at both ends and you'll come home doubly shattered.

There's no harm in that if you've got sufficient reservoirs, but it's bad news if in the process you're running your reservoirs dry. The time may come when you have to choose between propping up your image and trying to be flexible. The least painful course, and the one most easily rationalized, is usually to sacrifice flexibility.

So take the case of an inflexible man whom you're to encourage to be flexible. You say to him, 'I'm sorry, you've only brought me one option and I need to see a bit further than that.' So he goes away and comes back with the three options from which he derived the first. You persevere. 'Aren't there actually sixteen options, Harry? I'll just write them out for you and then you can go away and think about them.' When you do that, two things can happen.

On the one hand, Harry can turn brittle, frustrated and snappy. What's happening now is that his forceshield is becoming transparent and I'm seeing through to the real Harry underneath. And why? Well I've forced him to think about sixteen options, which is using up a lot of his intellectual energy, with the result that there's less energy left over for propping up the shield. The process needs caution. If Harry looks like being damaged by the experience, I must stop stretching him, acknowledge that he's never going to flex, and send him over to bought ledgers or whatever the equivalent department might be.

But it may turn out (and frequently does) that when Harry

is faced with sixteen options he starts to grow in stature. I can then draw the conclusion that this fellow might be going places; that he has a capacity to think things through and to have ideas. It is also likely that his real self and his compensatory image are closer together than he himself knew, and that all this time he has been expending energy unnecessarily in keeping the forceshield in place. Once Harry tumbles to that fact, he'll find himself with a lot of energy to spare and he could become more flexible overnight.

The good manager is a liberator, and I include both Pip and Anatole in that category. Exercising awareness, judgement, courage and flexibility, he will free his own staff from routine attitudes and courses, help them to exercise their real abilities, and expose them to the bracing wind of options and decisions. Which is the only way, in the end, for any enterprise to seize control of luck.

CHAPTER TEN

Management By Intuition

AWARENESS, JUDGEMENT, courage and flexibility: these, I believe, are the elemental qualities of a good manager. As I've tried to show, the more he can instil them into his own organization, as well as exhibiting them himself, the better he will manage his luck and the more successful he is likely to be.

Notice not just the four qualities but the order they're in. You can rank them differently depending on your criteria. I've chosen to deal with them chronologically, for this is the sequence in which they tend to be deployed.

Remember the MD of Babybounce? He becomes aware, first of all, that something very strange is happening to the pregnancy rate in the aftermath of that solar wind. He judges the data, perceives what is going on, and makes a decision to exploit the new situation. Now comes the courage. At some point he must knock on his chairman's door – or, more scarey still, face the full might of the board – and ask permission to boost production by a thousandfold.

'And why 1000 per cent, Mr Smith? Isn't that rather excessive?'

'Well, there's this solar wind, you see, and it's blowing across the earth and the result is –'

'Solar wind, Mr Smith?' The members of the board are exchanging knowing looks.

'Yes, and what this means is ...'

In the face of his colleagues' scepticism, our MD will need all the courage he can muster. Then, assuming he has won the day, he must start being incredibly flexible. Plans must be scrapped and remade; new plant must be built; more people must be employed; new processes may need to be developed and installed.

It's an outlandish example, I admit, but the same applies much nearer home.

I mentioned a couple of chapters ago that I was thinking of a new job. That possibility has moved a few stages closer in the course of the final work on this book. Originally I became aware of the opportunity through my own data-gathering methods. I've sat in judgement on what my awareness has told me, and that has been excruciating. It's a finely balanced decision: should I or shouldn't I? If I decide to jump, it will need a great deal of courage to go and see the Chairman of Glaxo and tell him I'm leaving. After that, assuming it all happens, my entire world will be turned upside down. I'll have to change my plans, my address, my attitudes, all sorts of things, and I know from experience how painful change can be.

So the order of events, again, is awareness, judgement, courage and flexibility.

You can, however, postulate a different order for the four qualities, based on the degree to which managers think they can deal with them.

Top of the list, again, comes awareness. Managers have all kinds of methods for making people aware: it's what information technology is all about, and every memo from every desk contributes, in theory, to the pool of corporate awareness. One stage down comes judgement. It's less easy to grapple with, but every manager knows he needs people who can exercise it. Courses and books abound on how to solve problems and make better decisions. The precise terms may differ, but you've probably seen both awareness and judgement mentioned in every management book you've read.

Now the ranking changes. In terms of what managers think they can do about them, flexibility and courage come way below the other two – and in that sequence.

You do sometimes see managers making efforts to remove blinkers and dig their people out of mental ruts, but the method tends to be exhortation ('Why can't you be more flexible?') rather than employing flexible people and building flexibility into the structure.

As for courage, it's very rarely mentioned. Interestingly, when people *fail* on courage, they're very quick to put it down to bad luck. Perhaps that's logical if courage is considered unalterable and you either have it or you don't. People can fail on awareness and they'll say, 'If only I had known ...' They can fall down on judgement and console themselves by exclaiming, 'If only I'd seen it differently ...' They can be inflexible and respond, 'If only I'd gone for the two o'clock train instead of the four o'clock ...' The battery of excuses is familiar: 'I didn't know ... I misjudged it ... I'm not changing now ...'

But lack of *courage*? For whatever reason, that's the last thing people admit to. Never in my managerial career have I heard someone say, 'I'm sorry I didn't do it, Mr Burke, I was a coward.'

Perhaps it goes back to childhood. You don't lose kudos with your peers if you're ignorant in the classroom, but you certainly do if you refuse a dare or you flinch first in a game of chicken. So cowardice it is that most quickly summons all the cant about bad luck. 'I lacked courage on this or that occasion, but subconsciously I can't admit it, so let's put it down to a phantom, uncontrollable, it-could-happen-to-anybody third party called Luck. I can then rest easy and needn't chastise myself for my failure.' If resting easy is the criterion, well and good. On the other hand, if you're serious about managing your luck, you ought at least to recognize your lack of courage even if you can't do much about it.

This brings us full circle to awareness. In truth, there is no

fixed order for these four qualities, for they bleed into each other and they turn out to be cyclical rather than linear.

Sometimes you will become aware only if you exercise a measure of courage or flexibility. Captain Kirk and his crewmates on Starship Enterprise are required 'to boldly go' before they can accomplish their fact-finding mission. (Courage first, awareness second.) It was only when Pip gave me confidence in my judgement, courage and flexibility that my awareness pores opened up and I found I could soak in data in a completely new way. Possibly the MD of Babybounce needs a measure of flexibility *before* he is brave as well as afterwards. And sometimes, when you've been as flexible as you can, courage is the only thing left and you must simply take a deep breath and jump in.

All the time, the four qualities are weaving in and out of one another. Once you have finished this book, you will simply have covered a small part of the awareness stage of managing your luck. You will then need to judge what you have read. Only you can do that; I can't do it for you. If the book has had any effect, you will probably have to change, which means being flexible. Just how flexible or courageous you choose to be is up to you.

In other words, having nearly reached the end, you are actually only at the beginning.

The more I reflect on the cyclical nature of the four qualities, the more convinced I am of the value of intuition.

'Intuition', like 'psychology', is one of those words that doesn't sit comfortably with most people's view of good management. 'We don't want businesses run by intuition,' they'll say. 'We want objectivity.' I have two responses. One is that intuition does not exclude objectivity, but rather embraces it. The other is that, in my experience, decisions made on intuition are often very sound ones.

Many times I have seen an expert in some field or other glance over a problem, suck his pencil for a moment and jot down the answer. His junior, following in his tracks, will pore over the documents, scribble furiously for ten minutes and finally arrive at the same conclusion. On the face of it, the expert has skipped the awareness stage and gone straight into judgement. Is he cheating? I think not. All he has done is play variations on the order. His awareness has been gleaned over decades, so he needn't delay now to re-acquire it. Long experience has given him the flexibility to discern the important patterns, to sort out what he already knows from what he doesn't, and to understand the implications of the data in front of him. He has also, back down the line, been brave enough to *trust* his intuition. Presumably there was a first time when he leaped to the answer rather than working it out from scratch. Having found that it works, he now has the confidence to do the same again.

Good management requires good communication: that I firmly believe. At the same time, I have to admit that on many issues I trust my intuition more than my ability to sort out and explain my reasons. It was Anatole Schwieger who first gave me access to my intuitions. He himself was highly intuitive. One of the reasons he appeared so chaotic was that most of his reasoning took place instantly and below the surface – perhaps even out of sight of his own consciousness. But under his guidance I learned to put greater weight on my intuition, and the process sent me all over the world doing strange and flexible things.

Intuition is not a stunt. It's a facility, born out of awareness, judgement, courage and flexibility, that in turn adds value to those qualities by enabling you to play tunes upon them. The intuitive person does not dispense with these four – they're elemental, as I've said – but he sometimes does some rather dazzling things with them. Or perhaps more commonly *she* dazzles. Because whilst it is a well known phenomenon that women act on intuition, usually quoted by men in a disparaging way, I do think women's right and left brain are better integrated, they are more intuitive and, most importantly, comfortable with their intuition. I once experienced a senior lady-manager (now a Director) hold out for a very bullish price on a product without fully being able to support it in her usual logical way. She had the day and was proved right. Later we were able to reinterpret the database with new data and found *why* she was right. It's just that she knew first!

The whole is greater than the sum of the parts. If awareness, judgement, courage and flexibility, taken in series, allow you to manage your luck, they'll do so all the better if you can play freely with the order and weave them into patterns. Therein lies real artistry in management.

CHAPTER ELEVEN

Getting It Together

YOU MANAGE luck by switching the ratio of that which you control against that which you abandon to fate – so you're managing more of your life and giving in to less of it. But even then you don't let go of the luck element. You create around it, snatching opportunity from the random events that fall in your path.

That is the core of my thesis, and I've tried to show how you as a manager can start to put it into effect. There's now one more piece to slot into place – yourself.

I've talked about extending your control over chance; about understanding and deploying your people; about being aware, exercising judgement, having courage and being flexible; and about how intuition can add value to those four qualities.

I've also touched on the kind of person you need to be for those qualities to be achievable. The manager of luck must be his own man, for you cannot take charge of events until you're in charge of yourself.

Your own man? What does that mean, and how do you achieve it? I could stop the book here and say, 'Sorry, you're either your own man, inherently capable of exercising these qualities, or you're not – that's the luck you're born with.'

But I won't. I resist the thought of giving ground to luck before I have to. So I ask the questions: What about my inbuilt characteristics, my genes? Do I take them as given, or can I extend my control internally as well as externally?

My first response is that managing myself is likely to be more difficult than managing other people. The tools I need to do it are the very tools I'm trying to analyze, and they're flawed. The law I'm trying to prove is the one I'm using to run the experiment, so objectivity is virtually impossible.

My second response is to try anyway. And the place to start, naturally, is with awareness. I may not be able to do much with what I find (that's another issue), but I can at least do everything possible to discover what's going on inside me. All right, there's the problem of objectivity, but with expert help I believe that problem can be overcome. I also believe it behoves every manager to make the attempt.

Let me at this point introduce Mrs Pat Herford, one of two people in my life (the other being Pip) who has instigated a quantum leap in my own psychological development. Trained in psychology at the Tavistock Institute, she's the kind of figure I have in mind when I talk about expert help. I met her when I was in my thirties, though my interest in the psychological aspects of management goes a few years further back, to the management course I attended at the Levinson Institute in Boston.

Half way through that course we had a free afternoon. We could do anything we liked, but it was pointed out that the Institute's own psychologists were available, if we wished, for further discussion on the relationship between psychology, awareness and self management. No-one took up the offer except me.

My first discovery was that psychologists never give you a lead.

'I wonder if you could sort me out on something that's bugging me,' I began.

'Tell me about it,' said a youthful, check-shirted American who looked more like a lumberjack than a psychologist. From my training as a salesman, I recognized the technique of the open-ended probe: no answers, just a constant rolling round of the questions.

I continued. 'This is the position I've reached,' I told him. 'I'm Vice President of a major American company. I'm on track to achieving my aspirations. I'm not unhappy, but not particularly happy either. I'm cheerful enough; I eat well; I sleep well; but I can't say I feel good about what I've done.'

'Oh yes?'

At the end of two hours I felt extremely foolish and no further forward. Usually I'm very objective. I know what I want to achieve and how much time is available to do it. I had gone in wanting hard data, and instead I'd got a sounding board. I recognize now that that's all a psychologist can be. He can't tell you anything about you because he doesn't know you. You tell yourself, using the impassivity of the other person as an anvil on which to shape your thoughts.

So it was that when I visited Pat Herford some years later, I went initially with a great deal of scepticism. In a little room in a house in St Albans I found a lady in her early 40s waiting to listen to me. She sat very calm and poised, hair slightly grey, eyes startlingly blue.

'Why have you come to see me?' she began.

'Here we go again,' I thought. 'Levinson Institute all over.' But faced with this lady's quiet charm, I started consciously discovering and piecing together all that I understood about myself from childhood but had never allowed to surface. The process was excruciating, and I was the only one who could do it. I had the data; she had none. All she could do was coax the information out and help me to interpret it.

Like all children, I was influenced more than I knew by my parents. As the Jesuits put it, 'Give me the child until he is seven and I will give you the man.' I understood that my parents had given me the ground rules for my life, but had never to that point defined precisely what those rules were. Under Pat's guidance, they emerged.

Be your own man. It's up to you to manage your opportunities. Nobody else will do anything for you. You are responsible for what you do – you and you only.

129

There's no point blaming your actions on circumstance or pressures. It's up to you.

You are responsible for your interaction with people. Don't expect them to carry the weight. You carry it.

And so on, and so on. It was during those interviews that Kipling's 'If' resurfaced and I remembered how it had permeated my entire childhood. So ingrained was the poem, I found I could recite it word for word even after all those years. Pat went away and read it.

'You see this as a template for manhood?' she enquired when we next met.

I agreed that I did, and that over the years I had striven to meet its standards.

'How do you rate yourself against it?'

'Sixty per cent,' I said.

'How do you arrive at 60?'

'I've checked myself against it,' I continued. 'Line by line, the things I can tick and the things I can't.'

She lowered the book with a sigh. 'The first thing I'll say is, it's a pretty exhausting course. If you can do all that, you won't be a man, my son, you'll be a saint. Furthermore, there are two statements in it I do not agree with and think are terribly dangerous.' She rarely made definitive statements, so this was startling.

I have thought about her objections a great deal since and have come to the conclusion that Pat is right and Kipling is wrong – on these two points at least.

The first is about truth.

If you can bear to hear the truth you've spoken Twisted by knaves ...

No. In all awareness and judgement there has to be absolute respect for the truth. It is not good enough to be so self-contained that distortions to the truth fall harmlessly about you and fail to provoke a reaction. You must react, or you might as well abandon the attempt to manage anything.

And beady-eyed awareness has to turn inwards as well as outwards.

'I haven't been a very good father to my children,' says a

member of the pact. 'Inevitable, I suppose. I'm Chairman now, you see, so what with jetting round the world all the time, living in aeroplanes, it's not surprising I hardly know them.'

The delusion is that career brilliance did for the relationship. Perhaps Mr Chairman has compensated for failure on the family front by becoming a workaholic – and a very successful workaholic. As long as that delusion persists, he denies himself that internal awareness without which he cannot properly take command of himself. That awareness can be painful to come by, but there is no managing your luck without it.

It seems we must re-work our definition of being your own man. As we last left it at the end of Chapter Three, being your own man is about taking responsibility for your own awareness and judgement and not selling your courage or flexibility to another party. But that does not mean making yourself an island and being accountable to no-one or nothing but yourself.

Being your own man means looking hard and long at things as they really are – at naked, undistorted truth – then allowing what you've seen to drive your actions. In other words, the man who is his own man is subservient only to the truth, having first sought it out as ruthlessly as he can. When the truth goes, everything goes, as every dictator knows. Perhaps that's why I'm so insistent on clear, crisp, accurate communication in my own organization.

Pat's other objection to Kipling was about people.
'If neither foes nor loving friends can hurt you,
And all men count with you but none too much ...
'That's not human,' she said. 'That's about making yourself a robot, insulating yourself and shutting your intellect and emotions in separate compartments. It's a discipline to stop you integrating yourself. You have to keep people at arm's length to behave like that.'

From what I know of Kipling, which is almost entirely gleaned from Birkenhead's biography, I'm not surprised to hear him speaking like this. He had a miserable childhood

that no doubt taught him to keep himself to himself. He was a sexist and closed-down type of man, though I like his writing. Like many incarcerated people, he found an outlet in being creative.

When my children were young, I taught them a credo based on Kipling, just as my father had taught me. I caught myself in time. It's not that I reject the poem: I'm with it all the way, other than on these two points. But I would now counsel my children to stay in touch with their emotions and not to fear them – and to stay in touch with people.

Having reworked the definition of being your own man under Pat's first objection, we must now redefine once more. To manage your luck it is not enough *only* to be your own man. Somehow you must be big enough to encompass *people* in your scheme of things. You need to be sufficiently integrated yourself to let people be people – to respect them as such – without letting go your hold on truth.

Ultimately as a manager you're doing two things. One: you're seeking out the truth and shaping your actions accordingly. Two: you're dealing with people and making things happen through people. Without the first you can build nothing. But without accommodating people, you build nothing either. No enterprise of yours can advance unless you're competent on both those levels. You must have both qualities to manage your luck. Unfortunately the two can be difficult to hold together. In real situations we continually slip from truth to people, from task to relationships, and back again.

When I was considering leaving Beecham I explored a number of options and through one of them found myself being interviewed for a senior management post within the industry. My first encounter was with the Personnel Manager. He irritated me at the very start by taking a flask from his drawer, pouring himself a cup of coffee and putting it back. In my house, I thought, visitors get offered a cup before I have one. Then he pulled out a form.

'Name?'

Well, this was the nth time that someone from the company

had sat me down and gone through the same list of questions. As he fussed about with his pen and straightened the papers on his desk, I began to detect that here was a man who had found a little corner, walled it off, climbed inside and set himself to play by the rules. I went along with him for a few moments as he fired more questions.

'Address? Age? What do you see yourself bringing to the job?'

I stopped him there and asked him who was actually choosing the candidate.

'Well, ultimately it's Mr B—,' he began.

'And where is Mr B—?'

'He's down the corridor. I'll be sending you along when we've finished.'

I said to him, 'You'll find me in reception when you're ready,' and walked out.

Mr B—, it turned out, was a direct, no-nonsense manager, who asked me to explain the trouble I had been causing on the fourth floor.

I apologized for upsetting his system, but pointed out that the Personnel Director was being insulting to the candidates – which wasn't very bright of him, because one of them would shortly be his boss. It's amazing how blinkered you can be when you're driven by your own craving for security.

For my part, I see this episode as an instance where I threw over the person to get to the truth – which here meant stopping the nonsense and getting down to the real business. If you like, my task-orientation overwhelmed my person-orientation – and I make no apology because I'm sure it was the right thing to do.

Eventually I did choose an option, to go to Searle as UK Marketing Director, and so found myself, a few weeks later, being sent off in style from Beecham where I'd been for twelve years. The marketing office was crammed with the colleagues I'd acquired in all those years, and the Marketing Director, Ed Stanford, gave a farewell speech.

'We'll miss John in a lot of different ways, but in one common way. From the highest to the lowest, we have all been exposed to the LBFs.'

There was laughter from around the room, and I was the only one who didn't understand the joke.

Ed went on to explain. 'LBFs – Long Bony Fingers. You've placed on the table your latest, most treasured belief and that terrible thing happens. Up come the LBFs and John checks them off. "That's fine," he says. "But what about A, B, C, D and E?" Then you realize the things you've still got to do.'

The speech was entirely good-humoured. Nevertheless, it worried me to think I was tearing through people's sensitivities with quite this effect. I had no idea I was doing it, and since then I have tried hard not to do it. There comes a time when you cannot throw over the person for the sake of truth. That's not to say you ignore the truth; you come at it by a different route.

I've mentioned the manager, desperate for affection, who passes on the ideas of his staff quite uncritically and inflicts enormous damage in the process. Let's replace him with a manager who respects both truth and people in equal measure. When a suggestion is brought to him, he will sit down and thrash it out with the people concerned. He won't put the obstacles first – that will simply demotivate – but he will work through to a result. Then he'll send the idea upstairs and give full credit to the person downstairs who produced it in the first place. Now, because it's a good idea, it gets the attention of the bosses and the manager can come back later and say, 'Your idea has been implemented. Well done.'

This is the much-loved manager, and he behaves this way, by and large, because he is integrated as a person. He is not preoccupied with feeding his own internal needs, so is unthreatened and can afford to be generous. He's a man who sees things as they are, for there's nothing in his psychology that needs to obfuscate. Being free himself, he can liberate his staff from psychological constrictions and raise their own levels of awareness, judgement, courage and flexibility. I also believe that the integrated man is more intuitive. I'm painting an ideal portrait, I acknowledge. I have glimpsed this man only on rare occasions, but I've seen enough to know that the integrated man makes the best manager.

Last question: How do you become integrated? Here I must rule off and admit that we've crossed out of this book into other books. My subject is management, not 'How to be Whole', and you must look elsewhere for the answer. But I offer you three observations to be going on with.

First, however you get your integration, you've got to have it. Every failure I've observed in awareness, judgement, flexibility and courage – and therefore every failure to manage luck – has come down to somebody's failure, somewhere, to be integrated as a person.

Next, you don't become integrated by following rules. Try to be an 'If' man and you'll explode.

Finally, the place to start is awareness: know your own psychology and take it from there.

Good luck – or let me say, good management.

LAST WORD

WHEN I started this book I was Chairman of Glaxo
Pharmaceuticals and expected still to be so when we
went to press.

It didn't happen. An opportunity cut across my path and I
decided to take it.

The timing was far from perfect and the decision to change
course was painful in the extreme. All change is loss, as we
have seen, but never in my career has the loss been this
serious. To leave Glaxo – high-profile, fast expanding, the
name behind some of the world's most successful medicines –
for the relative obscurity of Porton International seemed at
times like lunacy. Certainly there was no shortage of people
telling me so.

My answer is that this move has been a logical step in my
own management of luck. And, interestingly, the four key
qualities have all come into play.

I've been aware of Porton International for some time and
have watched it carefully as it has grown. I've been interested
not only in its pharmaceutical activities but also in its
exploration of biotechnology – notably biomedicals, bio-
processing, fermentation and plant design. At the same time,
Porton has been aware of me. Given that the pharmaceutical
industry is the most heavily audited and market-researched of
any, my record was not difficult to find.

Judging whether or not to move took several months of

deliberation. Should I stay where familiarity and experience seemed to offer a comfortable life, or pitch myself into a new environment where I'd need to build up my awarenesses almost from scratch? What swung it in the end was the tight team I saw at Porton, the lack of structural straight-jacketing, the refreshing absence of pacts and the opportunity to be in at the beginning of a brand new industry, one that could well overshadow the microchip for its importance and sheer breadth of application.

The judgemental process was just as difficult for Porton. A lot hung on Porton's management getting the appointment right. I trust they've done so!

Both sides have had to exercise courage and flexibility to get to this point. Going to see the Chairman of the Glaxo Group to tell him I was leaving was no easier than I had anticipated.

But now it's done and here I am. I won't say I was lucky to get the job, but I do consider myself fortunate.

Wish me good management, as I do you.